G. SCHIRMER'S COLLECTION OF OPERA LIBRETTOS

LA BOHÈME

Opera in Four Acts

Music by

Giacomo Puccini

Libretto by
GIUSEPPE GIACOSA and LUIGI ILLICA
(Based on "La Vie de Bohème" by Henry Murger)

English Version by
RUTH and THOMAS MARTIN

Ed. 2521

G. SCHIRMER, *Inc.*

Note

LA BOHÈME

La Bohème, fourth opera by Puccini (1858-1924) was the composer's second operatic success, preceded by two failures. Success had first come to the composer when he was 35 years old with the premiere of *Manon Lescaut* in 1893.

The first performance of *La Bohème* took place at the Teatro Regio in Turin on February 1, 1896, exactly three years after *Manon Lescaut,* in the same theater and under the same conductor, Arturo Toscanini, not yet 29 years of age.

The opera is based on *Scènes de la Vie de Bohème* by the Parisian novelist, Henri Murger — sketches of Bohemian life in Paris which first appeared in the journal *Le Corsair* between 1847 and 1849. The libretto marks Puccini's first collaboration with two writers Luigi Illica and Giuseppe Giacosa who, under his relentless supervision, were also to furnish the texts for *Tosca* and *Madama Butterfly.*

The opera was first performed in America by the Dal Conte company during a visit to Los Angeles in October 1897. It had its first performance at the Metropolitan Opera House in New York on December 26, 1900 with Melba as Mimi and Albert Seléza as Rodolfo.

THE STORY

ACT I. Among the smoking chimneys of 1830 Paris in their cheerless garret in the Latin Quarter, the near-destitute artist Marcello and poet Rodolfo try to keep warm on Christmas Eve by feeding the stove with pages from Rodolfo's drama. Before long they are joined by their roommates: Colline, a young philosopher, and Schaunard, a musician, who brings with him food, fuel and funds. As the four Bohemians celebrate their sudden good fortune, Benoit, the landlord, interrupts their gaiety with a bill for the rent. Plying the older man with wine, they encourage him to tell of his flirtations, then throw him out in pretended indignation. As his friends depart for further merrymaking, Rodolfo promises to join them later at the Café Momus. Alone and beginning to write, he is surprised by a knock at the door; this time the visitor turns out to be a pretty young neighbor, Mimi, whose candle has gone out on the drafty stairway. No sooner does the girl enter than she feels faint; after giving her a sip of wine to revive her, Rodolfo helps her to the door, relighting her candle. Suddenly Mimi realizes that she has lost her key; as the two search for it, their candles are blown out. In the moonlight the poet takes the girl's shivering hand to warm, telling her of his dreams. She responds by telling him how she lives alone in her lofty attic, embroidering flowers and waiting for the first kiss of April's sun. When Rodolfo's friends are heard from the distance, urging him to join them, he calls back that he will come along shortly and bring a friend. Expressing their new-found rapture, Mimi and Rodolfo embrace and leave for the café arm in arm.

ACT. II. Amid the shouts of hawkers selling their wares, Rodolfo buys Mimi a bonnet at a shop near the Café Momus. The toy-vendor Parpignol passes by, besieged by a group of eager children. After the poet introduces Mimi to his friends, they all select a table and order their meal. Soon Musetta, Marcello's high-spirited former sweetheart, makes a noisy entrance on the arm of her rich new admirer, the elderly Alcindoro; the ensuing tumult reaches its height when Musetta, trying to regain the painter's attention, sings a waltz about how popular she is wherever she goes. To get rid of Alcindoro, she complains that her shoe pinches, sending the old man off to fetch a new pair. The moment he is gone she falls into Marcello's open arms, and when the waiter comes with the bill, she tells him to charge everything to Alcindoro. A detachment of soldiers marches by the café and the Bohemians fall in behind, leaving Alcindoro, who rushes back with Musetta's new shoes, to face the bill.

ACT III. On the outskirts of Paris on a snowy morning, a customs officer admits farm women to the city with their butter and cheese. Late merrymakers can still be heard within a tavern, clinking their beer glasses. Soon Mimi wanders in, searching for the place where Marcello now lives with Musetta. When Marcello emerges, Mimi confesses to him that she is distraught over Rodolfo's incessant jealousy: it would be best for them to part. Rodolfo, who has been asleep in the tavern, is heard from within and Mimi quickly hides. The poet tells Marcello that he wants to separate from Mimi because she is so fickle, but, pressed for the real reason, he breaks down, saying that her illness can only grow worse in the poverty they live in. Overcome with tears, Mimi stumbles forth from her hiding place to bid her lover farewell, just as Marcello runs back into the tavern at a shriek of laughter from Musetta. While Mimi and Rodolfo exchange memories of their happiness, Musetta dashes from the tavern quarreling with Marcello, who has caught her flirting. The painter and his mistress part, shouting insults at one another, but Mimi and Rodolfo decide to remain together until spring.

v

ACT IV. Separated from their sweethearts, Rodolfo and Marcello lament their loneliness in the garret. Colline and Schaunard join them, bringing a meager meal; to lighten their spirits, the four friends stage a mock ball, which turns into a furious duel. At the height of the hilarity, Musetta bursts into the room to announce that Mimi is downstairs, so weak that she lacks the strength to climb the stairs. Rodolfo runs to assist her as Musetta tells how Mimi begged to be taken to Rodolfo so that she could die near him. When they have made the girl as comfortable as possible, Musetta leaves to sell her earrings to buy medicine and Colline goes off to pawn the coat that has served him so faithfully and so long. Left alone, Mimi wistfully reminds Rodolfo of their first happy days together, but she is seized by a violent fit of coughing. When the others return, Musetta gives Mimi a muff to warm her hands. As the girl peacefully drifts into death, Rodolfo lowers the blinds to soften the light. Suddenly Schaunard discovers that Mimi is dead. Rodolfo, the last to realize the fact, throws himself despairingly on her body, calling her name.

Courtesy of Opera News

CAST OF CHARACTERS

RODOLFO, a poet . . . . Tenor

SCHAUNARD, a musician . . . . Baritone

BENOIT, a landlord . . . . Bass

MIMI . . . . Soprano

PARPIGNOL . . . . Tenor

MARCELLO, a painter . . . . Baritone

COLLINE, a philosopher . . . . Bass

ALCINDORO, a councillor of state . . . . Bass

MUSETTA . . . . Soprano

CUSTOM HOUSE SERGEANT . . . . Bass

Townspeople, Soldiers, Servants, Children, Boys and Girls, Students, Working Girls, Gendarmes, etc.

TIME: About 1830 in Paris

SYNOPSIS OF SCENES

LA BOHÈME

QUADRO I

In Soffitta

Ampia finestra dalla quale si scorge una distesa di tetti coperti di neve. A destra un camino. Una tavola, un letto, un armadio, quattro sedie, un cavalletto da pittore con una tela sbozzata ed uno sgabello: libri sparsi, molti fasci di carte, due candelieri. Uscio nel mezzo, altro a sinistra.

Rodolfo e Marcello. Rodolfo guarda meditabondo fuori della finestra. Marcello lavora al suo quadro: "Il passagio del Mar Rosso."

MARCELLO

Questo Mar Rosso mi ammollisce e assidera come se addosso mi piovesse in stille.

(si allontana dal cavalletto per guardare il suo quadro)

Per vendicarmi, affogo un Faraone.

(a Rodolfo)

Che fai?

RODOLFO

Nei cieli bigi
guardo fumar dai mille
comignoli Parigi,
e penso a quel poltrone
di un vecchio caminetto ingannatore
che vive in ozio come un gran signore.

MARCELLO

Le sue rendite oneste
da un pezzo non riceve.

RODOLFO

Quelle sciocche foreste
che fan sotto la neve?

MARCELLO

Rodolfo, io voglio dirti un mio pensier profondo:
ho un freddo cane.

RODOLFO

Ed io, Marcel, non ti nascondo
che non credo al sudore della fronte.

MARCELLO

Ho diacciate
le dita quasi ancora le tenessi immollate
giù in quella gran ghiacciaia che è il cuore di Musetta.

RODOLFO

L'amore è un caminetto che sciupa troppo . . .

MARCELLO

e in fretta!

RODOLFO

dove l'uomo è fascina

MARCELLO

e la donna è l'alare . . .

RODOLFO

L'uno brucia in un soffio . . .

MARCELLO

e l' altro sta a guardare.

RODOLFO

Ma intanto qui si gela . . .

MARCELLO

e si muore d'inedia! . . .

RODOLFO

Fuoco ci vuole . . .

MARCELLO

(afferrando una sedia e facendo l'atto di spezzarla)

Aspetta . . . sacrifichiam la sedia!

(Rodolfo impedisce con energia l' atto di Marcello. Ad un tratto Rodolfo esce in un grido di gioia ad un' idea che gli è balenata.)

RODOLFO

Eureka!

(corre alla tavola e ne leva un voluminoso scartafaccio)

MARCELLO

Trovasti?

RODOLFO

Sì. Aguzza
l'ingegno. L'idea vampi in fiamma.

MARCELLO

Bruciamo il Mar Rosso?

LA BOHÈME

ACT I

A Garret

A large window, with a view of an expanse of snow-covered roofs. A stove, left. A table, a cupboard, a small bookcase, four chairs, an easel, a bed; some books, many bundles of paper, two candlesticks. Center, a door; left another.

Rodolfo and Marcello on-stage. Rodolfo looks thoughtfully out the window. Marcello works on his painting, "The Passage of the Red Sea."

MARCELLO

Whatever made me paint this old Red
  Sea to-day!
Even the sight of so much water chills
  me!

(stands back from the easel to look at his painting)

But in revenge a Pharoah has to drown!

(to Rodolfo)

Rodolfo!

RODOLFO

I am admiring millions of chimneys
  smoking
On all the roofs of Paris,
And thinking how that stove there,
That lazy, good-for-nothing piece of
  hardware,
Won't do a single thing to earn his
  board!

MARCELLO

Well, it must have been ages
Since last we paid his wages!

RODOLFO

And as much as we need him,
We're not able to feed him.

MARCELLO

Rodolfo I must make you
A most sincere confession:
It's freezing cold here.

RODOLFO

And I will grant you this concession,
That I am not exactly perspiring.

MARCELLO

All my fingers are frozen,
Just as cold and devoid of all feeling
As that enormous iceberg, the heart of
  Musetta!

RODOLFO

Yes, love is like a stove that is burning
  fiercely.

MARCELLO

. . . and quickly!

RODOLFO

Where the man is the tinder

MARCELLO

Which the woman ignited . . .

RODOLFO

While he burns to a cinder . . .

MARCELLO

She never gets excited.

RODOLFO

But meanwhile we are freezing . . .

MARCELLO

Almost dead of starvation!

RODOLFO

We need a fire . . .

MARCELLO

All right, then, this chair will be our
  salvation!

(grasping a chair, as if to break it up)

RODOLFO *(resists Marcello's plan)*

Eureka!

(an idea has struck him)

MARCELLO

You found it?

RODOLFO

Yes!

(takes a bulky manuscript from the table)

My genius is burning, aflame with inspiration!

MARCELLO

To burn my new painting?

1

RODOLFO

No. Puzza
la tela dipinta. Il mio dramma,
l' ardente mio dramma ci scaldi.

MARCELLO

(*con comico spavento*)

Vuoi leggerlo forse? Mi geli.

RODOLFO

No, in cener la carta si sfaldi
e l' estro rivoli ai suoi cieli.
Al secol gran danno minaccia . . .
È Roma in periglio!

MARCELLO

Gran cor!

RODOLFO

(*dà a Marcello una parte dello scartafaccio*)

A te l' atto primo.

MARCELLO

Qua.

RODOLFO

Straccia.

MARCELLO

Accendi.

(*Rodolfo batte un acciarino, accende
una candela e va al camino con Marcello: insieme danno fuoco a quella
parte dello scartafaccio buttato sul
focolare, poi entrambi prendone delle
sedie e seggono, riscaldandosi vol-
uttuosamente.*)

RODOLFO E MARCELLO

Che lieto baglior.

(*Entra Colline gettando con ira sulla
tavola un pacco di libri.*)

COLLINE

Già dell' Apocalisse appariscono i segni.
In giorno di Vigilia non s'accettano
pegni! . . .

(*si interrompe sorpreso*)

Una fiammata!

RODOLFO (*a Colline*)

Zitto, si dà il mio dramma . . .

COLLINE

. . . al fuoco.
Lo trovo scintillante.

RODOLFO

Vivo. (*il fuoco diminuisce*)

COLLINE

Ma dura poco.

RODOLFO

La brevità, gran pregio.

COLLINE

(*levandogli la sedia*)

Autore, a me la sedia.

MARCELLO

Quest'intermezzi fan morir d' inedia.
Presto.

RODOLFO

(*prende un' altra parte dello scartafaccio*)

Atto secondo.

MARCELLO

Non far sussurro.

(*Rodolfo straccia parte dello scartafaccio e lo getta sul camino; il fuoco
si ravviva.*)

COLLINE

Pensier profondo!

MARCELLO

Giusto color!

RODOLFO

In quell' azzurro guizzo languente
sfuma un' ardente scena d' amor.

COLLINE

Scoppietta un foglio.

MARCELLO

Là c' eran baci!

RODOLFO

(*getta al fuoco il rimanente dello
scartafaccio*)

Tre atti or voglio d' un colpo udir.

COLLINE

Tal degli audaci l'idea s' integra.

TUTTI

Bello in allegra vampa svanir.

(*La fiamma diminuisce.*)

MARCELLO

Oh! Dio . . . già s' abbassa la fiamma.

COLLINE

Che vano, che fragile dramma!

RODOLFO
No, who could endure the aroma!
But my drama,
Its passionate ardor will warm us both!

MARCELLO (*with comic terror*)
You don't mean to read it? How awful!

RODOLFO
No, the paper will crumble to ashes,
The Muse will return to Olympus,
A masterpiece goes to perdition!
The loss is prodigious!

MARCELLO
How true!

RODOLFO
(*gives Marcello part of the manuscript*)
Begin with the first act.

MARCELLO
Right!

RODOLFO
Tear it!

MARCELLO
You light it.
(*Rodolfo lights a candle, and goes to
the stove with Marcello; together
they set fire to a part of the manuscript thrown into the grate; then
both draw up their chairs and sit
down, warming themselves with ex-
quisite delight.*)

RODOLFO
How cozy and bright.

MARCELLO
A heart-warming sight!
(*Colline enters, angrily throws on the
table a bundle of books.*)

COLLINE
Could it be that Judgment Day is
dawning!
On Christmas Eve the broker shops
won't do any pawning!
(*stops in surprise on seeing the fire in
the stove*)
I must be dreaming!

RODOLFO (*to Colline*)
Quiet! There goes my drama.

COLLINE
To blazes.
It seems to be enlightening!

RODOLFO
Brilliant! (*The fire dies down.*)

COLLINE
And very short.

RODOLFO
Brevity is an asset.

COLLINE
(*takes the chair from Rodolfo*)
I have your kind permission!

MARCELLO
I cannot stand a boring intermission!
Hurry!

RODOLFO
(*takes another part of the manuscript*)
Here is the second act!

MARCELLO
Don't breathe a whisper!
(*Rodolfo tears up the manuscript and
throws it into the stove; the fire
revives.*)

COLLINE
What words of wisdom!

MARCELLO
Right to the point!

RODOLFO
Amid these bluish flickering flames
A passionate love-scene goes up in
smoke!

COLLINE
It pops and crackles!

MARCELLO
There! Those were kisses!

RODOLFO
(*throws the rest of the manuscript into
the fire*)
Acts three to five at a single stroke!

COLLINE
Thus is a poet's dream accomplished.

ALL THREE
Nothing so gay as death on the pyre!

(*The fire dies down.*)

MARCELLO
Already the drama is ending.

COLLINE
It's finished, there's no use pretending!

MARCELLO

Già scricchiola, increspasi, muore.

(*Il fuoco è spento*)

COLLINE E MARCELLO

Abasso, abasso l' autore!

(*Dalla porta di mezzo entrano due garzoni, portando l' uno provviste di cibi, bottiglie di vino, sigari, e l' altro un fascio di legna.*)

RODOLFO

Legna!

MARCELLO

Sigari!

COLLINE

Bordò!

TUTTI E TRE

Le dovizie d' una fiera
il destin ci destinò.

(*i garzoni partono*)

SCHAUNARD

(*entra con aria di trionfo, gettando a terra alcuni scudi*)

La Banca di Francia
per voi si sbilancia.

COLLINE

Raccatta, raccatta!

MARCELLO (*incredulo*)

Son pezzi di latta! . . .

SCHAUNARD

(*mostrandogli uno scudo*)

Sei sordo? . . . Sei lippo?
Quest' uomo chi è?

RODOLFO (*inchinadosi*)

Luigi Filippo! M' inchino al mio Re!

TUTTI

Sta Luigi Filippo ai nostri piè!

(*Schaunard vorrebbe raccontare la sua fortuna*)

SCHAUNARD

(*raccattando gli scudi*)

Or vi dirò: quest' oro, o meglio, argento
ha la sua brava istoria . . .

MARCELLO

Riscaldiamo il camino!

COLLINE

Tanto freddo ha sofferto!

SCHAUNARD

Un inglese, un signor, lord o milord
che sia, volea un musicista . . .

MARCELLO

(*gettando via i libri di Colline dalla tavola*)

Via! Prepariamo la tavola!

SCHAUNARD

Io? volo!

RODOLFO

L' esca dov' è?

COLLINE

Là.

MARCELLO

Qua.

(*Accendono un gran fuoco nel camino*)

SCHAUNARD

E mi presento.
M' accetta gli domando . . .

(*Mettono a posto le vivande*)

MARCELLO

Pasticcio dolce!

COLLINE

Arrosto freddo!

SCHAUNARD

A quando le lezioni? . . .
Mi presento
M'accetta e gli domando:
A quando le lezioni?
Risponde: "Incominciam!"
"Guardare!" (e un pappagallo
m'addita al primo pian),
poi soggiunge: "Voi suonare
finchè quello morire!" E fu
così:
Suonai tre lunghi dì . . .

RODOLFO

Fulgida folgori la sala splendida.

MARCELLO

(*mette le due candele accese sul tavolo*)

Or le candele!

COLLINE

Pasticcio dolce!

MARCELLO

It shrivels and crumbles away!

(*The fire goes out.*)

MARCELLO AND COLLINE

Fiasco! Fiasco! Down the play!

(*From the center door two boys enter, one carrying food, bottles of wine, and cigars, the other a fagot of wood.*)

RODOLFO

Firewood!

MARCELLO

Burgundy!

COLLINE

Cigars!

ALL THREE

Well, it looks as if we'd celebrate this Christmas after all!

SCHAUNARD

(*enters with an air of triumph*)

I herewith provide us
With all the gold of Midas!

(*Throws some coins on the floor. The two boys leave.*)

COLLINE

We're rolling in money!

MARCELLO (*incredulously*)

You're not very funny!

SCHAUNARD

(*showing Marcello a coin*)

You stupid! Look closer!
You notice this face?

RODOLFO (*bowing*)

We bow to his majesty's bountiful grace.

ALL FOUR

Why, King Louis Philippe in our lowly place!

SCHAUNARD

(*continues to recount his good luck*)

Now you must hear:
This gold here, or better silver, has quite a striking story.

MARCELLO

I must tend to my stoking!

COLLINE

Get the poor fellow smoking!

SCHAUNARD

Seems a rich English peer,
Lord, or Milord or something,
Required a musician . . .

MARCELLO

(*pushing Colline's books off the table*)

Off, Let's prepare the festivities!

SCHAUNARD

I fly there.

RODOLFO

Where is the flint?

COLLINE

There!

MARCELLO

Here!

(*They build up a great fire in the stove.*)

SCHAUNARD

I make my entrance,
I ask him "How about it,

(*They arrange the food on the table.*)

MARCELLO

Delicious pastry!

COLLINE

Excellent roast-beef!

SCHAUNARD

When shall we start the lessons?"
I make my entrance,
I ask him "How about it,
When shall we start the lessons?"
He answers,

(*imitating an English accent in the words in italics*)

"*Right away!*"
"*Look here*" says he, and points to a parrot in a cage;
Then he added, "*Just keep right on playing
Till he expires!*"
And so it was; I played for three whole days.

RODOLFO

Let's have a festival illumination!

MARCELLO

(*places two lighted candles on the table*)

Here are the candles!

COLLINE

Delicate pastry!

SCHAUNARD

Allora usai l'incanto
di mia presenza bella,
di mia presenza bella . . .
Affascinai l'ancella . . .

MARCELLO

Mangiar senza tovaglia?

RODOLFO
(*leva un giornale di tasca*)

Un' idea! . . .

MARCELLO, COLLINE

Il Costituzional!

RODOLFO

Ottima carta . . .
Si mangia e si divora un' appendice!

SCHAUNARD

Gli propinai prezzemolo . . .
(*dispongono il giornale come una to-*
vaglia)
Lorito allargò l'ali,
Lorito il becco aprì,
Un poco di prezzemolo,
Da Socrate morì!
(*Vedendo che nessuno gli bada, afferra*
Colline che gli passa vicino con un
piatto.)

COLLINE

Chi?!

SCHAUNARD
(*urlando indispettito*)

Che il diavolo vi porti tutti quanti!
Ed or che fate?
No! Queste cibarie
sono la salmeria
pei dì futuri
tenebrosi e oscuri,
Pranzare in casa il dì della Vigilia.
Mentre il Quartier Latino le sue vie
addobba di salsicce e leccornie?
Quando un olezzo di frittelle imbalsama
le vecchie strade?
Là le ragazze cantano contente . . .

RODOLFO, MARCELLO, COLLINE

La vigilia di Natal!

SCHAUNARD

Ed han per eco ognuna uno studente!
(*solenne*)

Un po' di religione, o miei signori:
Si beva in casa, ma si pranzi fuor!
(*Bussano alla porta: s' arrestano stup-*
efatti.)

BENOIT

Si può?

MARCELLO

Chi è là?

BENOIT

Benoit.

MARCELLO

Il padrone di casa!

SCHAUNARD

Uscio sul muso.

COLLINE (*grida*)

Non c' è nessuno.

SCHAUNARD

È chiuso.

BENOIT (*di fuori*)

Una parola.

SCHAUNARD
(*dopo essersi consultato cogli altri, va*
ad aprire)

Sola!

BENOIT
(*entra sorridente: vede Marcello e mos-*
trandogli una carta dice)

Affitto!

MARCELLO
(*con esagerata premura*)

Olà! Date una sedia.

RODOLFO

Presto.

BENOIT (*schermendosi*)

Non occorre. Vorrei . . .

SCHAUNARD
(*insistendo con dolce violenza lo fa*
sedere)

Segga.

MARCELLO

Vuol bere? (*gli versa del vino*)

BENOIT

Grazie.

RODOLFO E COLLINE

Tocchiamo.

(*Tutti bevono*)

SCHAUNARD

But then I started to flirt
With the parlor Cinderella,
The parlor Cinderella.
Sub rosa, a cappella . . .

MARCELLO

A bare table to eat on?

RODOLFO

(taking a newspaper out of his pocket)
Here you are!

MARCELLO AND COLLINE

The Paris Evening Star!

RODOLFO

What could be better!
You eat as you digest the latest gossip!

SCHAUNARD

I treat the bird to arsenic.
(They spread the newspaper like a
    tablecloth.)
My polly spreads his pinions,
His beak he opened wide.
A little pinch of arsenic —
Like Socrates, he died!
(seeing that nobody pays attention,
    grasps Colline as he passes with a
    plate)

COLLINE

Who?

SCHAUNARD (irritably)

I hope the devil takes you altogether!
What are you doing? No!
All these provisions
We'll put inside our larder,
They will be welcome
When the times are harder.
On Christmas Eve we cannot linger
    indoors,
While all the markets of the Latin
    Quarter
Are filled with food that makes your
    palate water!
When the aroma of baked apples
Deliciously pervades the alleys!
Where all the young girls merrily are
    singing

RODOLFO, MARCELLO, COLLINE

Christmas carols through the night!

SCHAUNARD

Each has a student following her foot-
    steps!

(solemnly)

No more of this blaspheming,
My friends, I beg you.
We're drinking indoors,
But we're dining out!
(Two knocks are heard at the door.)

BENOIT

Permit me?

MARCELLO

Who is there?

BENOIT

Benoit!

MARCELLO

O good heavens, the landlord!

SCHAUNARD

Lock the door quickly!

COLLINE

We're out!

SCHAUNARD

It's bolted!

BENOIT (back-stage)

One word only!

SCHAUNARD

(after consulting his friends, goes to
    open the door)
One!

BENOIT

(enters, smiling, and shows a paper to
    Marcello)
Rent!

MARCELLO

(receiving him with great cordiality)
Hello! Won't you sit down, sir?

RODOLFO

Quickly.

BENOIT

Please don't bother, I only . . . (excus-
    ing himself)

SCHAUNARD

(gently insisting that he sit down)
Be seated.

MARCELLO

(offers Benoit a glass of wine)
A drink?

BENOIT

Thank you!

RODOLFO AND COLLINE

Good health, sir.

(They all drink.)

SCHAUNARD

Beva!

RODOLFO

Tocchiam!

BENOIT

Quest'è l' ultimo trimestre . . .

MARCELLO

(con ingenuità)

N'ho piacere.

BENOIT

E quindi . . .

SCHAUNARD (interrompendolo)

Ancora un sorso.

BENOIT

Grazie.

RODOLFO

Tocchiam!

COLLINE

Tocchiam!

I QUATTRO (toccando con Benoit)

Alla sua salute!

(Tutti bevono.)

BENOIT (a Marcello)

A lei ne vengo
perchè il trimestre scorso mi promise . . .

MARCELLO

(mostrando a Benoit gli scudi che sono
sulla tavola)

Promisi ed or mantengo.

RODOLFO (piano a Marcello)

Che fai?

SCHAUNARD (come sopra)

Sei pazzo?

MARCELLO

(a Benoit, senza badare ai due)

Ha visto? Or via
resti un momento in nostra compagnia
Dica: quant' anni ha,
caro signor Benoit?

BENOIT

Gli anni? . . . Per carità!

RODOLFO

Su e giù la nostra età.

BENOIT

Di più, molto di più.
(Mentre fanno chiacchierare Ben...
gli riempiono il bicchiere appena e...
l' ha vuotato.)

COLLINE

Ha detto su e giù.

MARCELLO

L'altra sera al Mabil.
L'han colto in peccato d'amor!

BENOIT (inquieto)

Io?

MARCELLO

Al Mabil, l'altra sera
l'han colto. Neghi!

BENOIT

Un caso.

MARCELLO (lusingandolo)

Bella donna!

BENOIT

(mezzo brillo, con subito moto)

Ah! Molto.

SCHAUNARD

(gli batte una mano sulla spalla)

Briccone!

RODOLFO

Briccone!

COLLINE

Seduttore!

SCHAUNARD

Briccone!

RODOLFO

Briccone!

MARCELLO

Una quercia! . . . un cannone!

BENOIT

Eh! Eh!

RODOLFO

L' uomo ha buon gusto.

MARCELLO

Il crin ricciuto e fulvo.

SCHAUNARD

Briccone!

MARCELLO

Ei gongolava arzillo, pettoruto.

BENOIT (ringalluzzito)

Son vecchio, ma robusto.

SCHAUNARD
Another!

RODOLFO
Your health!

BENOIT
I have come here to remind you . . .

MARCELLO (*innocently*)
Yes, I know it.

BENOIT
And therefore . . .

SCHAUNARD (*interrupting him*)
Let's have another!

BENOIT
Thank you!

RODOLFO
A toast!

COLLINE
A toast!

RODOLFO
MARCELLO, SCHAUNARD, COLLINE
(*rising they all touch glasses with Benoit*)
Here's to Mister Benoit!
(*They sit and drink.*)

BENOIT (*to Marcello*)
I came because when your last month's rent was owing,—
You had promised . . .

MARCELLO
(*showing Benoit the money on the table*)
I never break a promise.

RODOLFO (*aside to Marcello*)
What this?

SCHAUNARD (*aside to Marcello*)
You're crazy?

MARCELLO
(*to Benoit, disregarding the two*)
You saw it? And now just stay a moment
In our congenial circle
Tell me how old you are,—
Dear Mister Benoit?

BENOIT
How old? For Heaven's sake!

RODOLFO
Our own age, more or less?

BENOIT
Much more, very much more.
(*While they make Benoit chatter, they fill up his glass as soon as he has emptied it.*)

COLLINE
He only made a guess.

MARCELLO
Sunday evening, at a certain tavern,
You were seen making love!

BENOIT (*uneasily*)
I?

MARCELLO
No one else.
With my own eyes I saw you. Admit it!

BENOIT
It's true, but . . .

MARCELLO (*flattering him*)
Gorgeous woman!

BENOIT (*suddenly half-drunk*)
A darling!

SCHAUNARD
(*slaps him on the shoulder*)
You rascal!

RODOLFO
You Don Juan!

COLLINE
He's a smart one!

SCHAUNARD
Seducer!

RODOLFO
Seducer!

MARCELLO
You should see her! What a woman!

BENOIT
Ha! Ha!

RODOLFO
He is an expert.

MARCELLO
A veritable Venus!

SCHAUNARD
Old fox!

MARCELLO
With youthful fire he returned her ardent kisses.

BENOIT (*preening himself*)
I'm old, but don't show it.

COLLINE, SCHAUNARD E RODOLFO
Ei gongolava arzuto e pettorillo.

MARCELLO
E a lui cedea la femminil virtù.

BENOIT
(*in piena confidenza*)
Timido in gioventù
Ora me ne ripago! Si sa,
È uno svago qualche . . .
Donnetta allegra . . .
E un po' . . .
Non dico una balena
O un mappamondo
O un viso tondo
Da luna piena,
Ma magra, proprio magra,
No, poi no!
Le donne magre
Son grattacapi
E spesso sopracapi . . .
E son piene di doglie,
Per esempio: mia moglie . . .

MARCELLO
(*si alza: gli altri lo imitano*)
Quest'uomo ha moglie
e sconcie voglie
ha nel cor!

SCHAUNARD, COLLINE
Orror!

RODOLFO
E ammorba, e appesta
la nostra onesta magion!

SCHAUNARD, COLLINE
Fuor!

MARCELLO
Si abbruci dello zucchero!

COLLINE
Si discacci il reprobo!

SCHAUNARD
È la morale offesa . . .

BENOIT
(*allibito, tenta inutilmente di parlare*)
Io di . . .

COLLINE
Silenzio!

SCHAUNARD
Che vi scaccia!

MARCELLO
Silenzio!

RODOLFO
Silenzio!
(*circondano Benoit, e lo spingono poco
a poco verso la porta*)

BENOIT
Miei signori . . .

MARCELLO, SCHAUNARD
COLLINE, RODOLFO
Silenzio! Via, signore! Via di qua!
(*Benoit è cacciato fuori*)
E buona sera a vostra signori! . . .
(*ritornando nel mezzo della scena*)
Ah! Ah! Ah!

MARCELLO
Ho pagato il trimestre.

SCHAUNARD
Al Quartiere Latin ci attende Momus.

MARCELLO
Viva chi spende!

SCHAUNARD
Dividiamo il bottin!
(*si dividono gli scudi sul tavolo*)

RODOLFO
Dividiam!

COLLINE
Dividiam!

MARCELLO
(*presentando uno specchio rotto a Col-
line*)
Là ci son beltà scese dal cielo.
Or che sei ricco, bada alla decenza!
Orso, ravviati il pelo.

COLLINE
Farò la conoscenza
la prima volta d' un barbitonsore.
Guidatemi al ridicolo
oltraggio d' un rasoio.

SCHAUNARD
Andiam!

MARCELLO
Andiam!

SCHAUNARD
Andiam!

RODOLFO, SCHAUNARD, COLLINE

With youthful fire he answered her caresses.

MARCELLO

He made her yield, the lovely child of joy!

BENOIT (confiding fully)

I was a timid boy,
Now I am getting even! You know
I've a certain weakness.
For certain ladies . . .
You see . . .
Not that I like them portly
Or downright tubby,
Or even chubby,
A blooming full-moon.
But skinny, lean and skinny,
No, sir, no!
When they are skinny,
They are malicious,
And sometimes even vicious.
I don't care for their kisses,
Least of all for—my Missus! . . .

MARCELLO

(Rises. The others follow his example.)
This man is married and leads a scandalous life!

SCHAUNARD AND COLLINE

Disgrace!

RODOLFO

This man infects and corrupts our impeccable home!

SCHAUNARD AND COLLINE

Out!

MARCELLO

We'll have to disinfect the place!

COLLINE

Drive the wretched sinner out!

SCHAUNARD

Our morals are offended!

BENOIT

One word . . . I say . . .

COLLINE

Keep quiet!

SCHAUNARD

We expel you!

MARCELLO

Be quiet!

RODOLFO

Be quiet!
(They push Benoit gradually towards the door.)

BENOIT

Only listen . . .

MARCELLO,
SCHAUNARD, COLLINE AND RODOLFO

Be quiet! Quickly out of here!
(Pushing Benoit out the door.)
Out you go!
And give your lady our very best regards.
(laughing, returning to center stage)
Ha, ha, ha, ha!

MARCELLO

Go and look for your money!

SCHAUNARD

Now it's time to be off for Café Momus!

MARCELLO

Spending our money!

SCHAUNARD

Let's divide all the spoils.
(They divide the money on the table.)

RODOLFO

Right away!

COLLINE

Right away!

MARCELLO

(holding up a cracked mirror to Colline)
There you will find girls, heavenly creatures.
Now that you're wealthy, bow before convention!
Bear! Get yourself a trimming.

COLLINE

I shall for the first time receive attention
From a barber's scissors.
Escort me to the ludicrous excesses of the razor.
Come on!

SCHAUNARD

Let's go!

MARCELLO

Let's go!

SCHAUNARD

Let's go!

COLLINE
Andiam!

RODOLFO
Io resto per terminar
l'articolo di fondo del *Castoro*.

MARCELLO
Fa presto.

RODOLFO
Cinque minuti. Conosco il mestier.

COLLINE
T'aspetterem dabbasso dal portier.

MARCELLO
Se tardi udrai che coro!

RODOLFO
Cinque minuti.

SCHAUNARD
Taglia corta la coda al tuo *Castor*.
(*Marcello, Schaunard, Colline escono e
scendono la scala.*)

MARCELLO (*di fuori*)
Occhio alla scala. Tieni
alla ringhiera.

RODOLFO
(*sempre sull' uscio*)
Adagio.

COLLINE (*di fuori*)
È buio pesto!

SCHAUNARD
Maledetto portier!
(*rumore d' uno che ruzzola*)

COLLINE
Accidenti!

RODOLFO
Colline, sei morto?

COLLINE (*dal basso*)
Non ancor.

MARCELLO (*dal basso*)
Vien presto.
(*Rodolfo chiude l' uscio, depone il
lume, poi siede e si mette a scrivere
ma non trovando alcuna idea, s' in-
quieta, straccia il foglio e getta via
la penna.*)

RODOLFO
Non sono in vena.
(*si bussa alla porta*)
Chi è là?

MIMÌ (*di fuori*)
Scusi.

RODOLFO
Una donna!

MIMÌ
Di grazia, mi s'è spento il lume.

RODOLFO
(*corre ad aprire*)
Ecco.

MIMÌ
(*sull' uscio, con un lume spento in
mano ed una chiave*)
Vorrebbe . . . ?

RODOLFO
S' accomodi un momento.

MIMÌ
Non occorre.

RODOLFO (*insistendo*)
La prego, entri.

MIMÌ
(*entra: è presa da soffocazione*)
Ah!

RODOLFO
Si sente male?

MIMÌ
No . . . nulla.

RODOLFO
Impallidisce!

MIMÌ (*presa da tosse*)
Il respir . . . Quelle scale . . .
(*Sviene e Rodolfo è appena a tempo di
sorreggerla ed adagiarla su di una
sedia, mentre dalle mani di Mimì
cadono e candeliere e chiave.*)

RODOLFO (*imbarazzato*)
Ed ora come faccio?
(*va a prendere dell' acqua e ne spruzza
il viso di Mimì*)
Così.
(*guardandola con grande interesse*)
Che viso d'ammalata
Si sente meglio?

COLLINE

Let's go!

RODOLFO

I'm staying, I have to write
A critical report for next month's
    "Beaver."

MARCELLO

Then hurry.

RODOLFO

I will be with you in no time at all . . .

COLLINE

We'll wait for you downstairs in the
    hall.

MARCELLO

If you are late you'll hear us!
(*Marcello, Schaunard, and Collins go
    out and descend the staircase.*)

RODOLFO

Five minutes only.

SCHAUNARD

Better shorten your Beaver's wordy tail!

MARCELLO (*off-stage*)

Look where you're going,
Keep along the railing.

RODOLFO (*on the landing*)

Be careful!

COLLINE (*off-stage*)

Infernal darkness!

SCHAUNARD

I am risking my neck!
(*Noise of someone falling.*)

COLLINE

I have done it!

RODOLFO

Colline, are you dead?

COLLINE

(*In the distance, from the bottom of the
    stairs.*)
No, not quite.

MARCELLO (*further away*)

Come soon!
(*Rodolfo closes the door, puts the can-
    dle down, then sits down and pre-
    pares to write. Writes, breaks off,
    thinks, writes again.*)

RODOLFO

I'm not inspired.
        (*a timid knock at the door*)
Who's there?

MIMI (*off-stage*)

Excuse me.

RODOLFO

Who can that be?

MIMI

Forgive me. Will you light my candle?

RODOLFO

    (*runs to open the door*)
There now.

MIMI

(*at the door, holding an extinguished
    candle and a key*)
Allow me . . .

RODOLFO

Won't you stay a moment?

MIMI

Please don't bother.

RODOLFO (*insistently*)

Come in please, won't you?

MIMI

(*enters, but suddenly is seized with a
    coughing spell*)

RODOLFO

You're feeling ill?

MIMI

No . . . nothing. (*coughing*)

RODOLFO

But you are trembling.

MIMI

Oh, these stairs, they exhaust me . . .
(*Faints, and Rodolfo hardly has time to
    support her and lead her to a chair,
    while the candlestick and key drop
    from her hand.*)

RODOLFO (*embarrassed*)

What can I do to help her?
I know!
(*goes to get water, and sprinkles it on
    her face*)
(*looking at her with deep interest*)
How pale and wan her face is!
Do you feel better?

MIMÌ (*rinviene*)

Sì.

RODOLFO

Qui c' è tanto freddo. Segga vicino
al fuoco.
(*Mimì fa cenno di no*)
Aspetti . . . un po' di vino.

MIMÌ

Grazie.

RODOLFO

(*le dà il bicchiere e le versa da bere*)
A lei.

MIMÌ

Poco, poco.

RODOLFO

Così.

MIMÌ

Grazie. (*beve*)

RODOLFO (*ammirandola*)

(Che bella bambina!)

MIMÌ

(*levandosi, cerca il suo candeliere*)
Ora permetta
che accenda il lume. È tutto passato.

RODOLFO

Tanta fretta?

MIMÌ

Sì.
(*Rodolfo accende il lume di Mimì e
gliela consegna*)

MIMÌ

(*s'avvia per uscire*)
Grazie. Buona sera.

RODOLFO

(*l' accompagna fino sull' uscio, poi ritorna subito al lavoro*)
Buona sera.

MIMÌ

(*esce, poi riappare sull' uscio*)
Oh! sventata!
La chiave della stanza!
Dove l' ho lasciata?

RODOLFO

Non stia sull' uscio;
il lume vacilla al vento.
(*Il lume di Mimì si spegne.*)

MIMÌ

Oh Dio! Torni ad accenderlo.

RODOLFO

(*accorre colla sua candela per riaccen-
dere quella di Mimì, ma avvicinandosi alla porta anche il suo lume si
spegne e la camera rimane buia*)
Oh Dio! Anche il mio s' è spento.

MIMÌ

Ah! E la chiave ove sarà?

RODOLFO

Buio pesto!

MIMÌ

Disgraziata!

RODOLFO

Ove sarà?

MIMÌ (*con grazia*)

Importuna è la vicina . . .

RODOLFO

Ma le pare!

MIMÌ

Importuna è la vicina

RODOLFO

Cosa dice, ma le pare!

MIMÌ

Cerchi!

RODOLFO

Cerco!
(*si trova presso la porta e la chiude*)

MIMÌ

Ove sarà?

RODOLFO

(*la trova e la intasca*)
Ah!

MIMÌ

L' ha trovata?

RODOLFO

No!

MIMÌ

Mi parve . . .

RODOLFO

. . . in verità!

MIMI (*revives*)
Yes!

RODOLFO
It is very cold here.
Warm yourself by the fire.
(*Mimi declines with a gesture.*)
One moment. A little wine now.

MIMI
Thank you!

RODOLFO
To you!
(*gives her a glass and pours out some wine*)

MIMI
Just a little!

RODOLFO
Like this?

MIMI
Thank you! (*She drinks.*)

RODOLFO (*admiring her*)
She really is lovely!

MIMI
(*rising, she looks for her candle-stick*)
Now may I ask you to light my candle.
I feel much better.

RODOLFO
Such a hurry?

MIMI
Yes.
(*Rodolfo sees the candlestick on the floor, picks it up, lights it, and hands it to Mimi.*)

MIMI (*ready to go*)
Thank you! And good evening.

RODOLFO
(*accompanies her to the door*)
You are welcome.
(*returns at once to the table*)

MIMI (*off-stage*)
Oh! How dreadful, how dreadful,
(*reentering, and stopping on the threshold of the door, which remains open*)
I cannot find my door-key,
I am so forgetful!

RODOLFO
Don't stay so near the doorway;
The wind is too strong for your candle,
(*Mimi's light goes out.*)

MIMI
Good Heaven's! Light it once more for me.

RODOLFO
(*Runs with his candle, his light goes out too; the room is in darkness.*)
Oh, my! Now I have none either!

MIMI
Ah! and my key, where can it be?

RODOLFO
(*finds himself near the door and shuts it*)
And it's dark here!

MIMI
I am sorry!

RODOLFO
Where can it be?

MIMI (*apologetically*)
Oh, what trouble I am causing!

RODOLFO
It is nothing . . .

MIMI
Oh, what trouble I am causing!

RODOLFO
It is nothing, I assure you!

MIMI
Help me!

RODOLFO
Gladly!
(*knocks against the table, puts his candlestick down, and searches for the key with his hands on the floor*)

MIMI
Where can it be?

RODOLFO
(*finds the key and puts it in his pocket*)
Ah!

MIMI
Did you find it?

RODOLFO
No!

MIMI
I thought you . . .

RODOLFO
I thought so, too!

MIMÌ

(cerca a tastoni)

Cerca?

RODOLFO

(finge di cercare, ma guidato dalla voce e dai passi di Mimì, tenta avvicinarsi ad essa)

Cerco!

(Mimì china a terra, cerca sempre tastoni: in questo momento Rodolfo si è avvicinato ed abbassandosi esso pure, la sua mano incontra quella di Mimì)

MIMÌ

Ah!

RODOLFO

(tenendo la mano di Mimì)

Che gelida manina,
se la lasci riscaldar.
Cercar che giova! Al buio non si trova.
Ma per fortuna è una notte di luna,
e qui la luna l' abbiamo vicina.
Aspetti signorina,
le dirò con due parole
chi son, chi son e che faccio,
come vivo.
Vuole?
Chi son, chi son?
Sono un poeta. Che cosa faccio?
Scrivo. E come vivo?
Vivo.
In povertà mia lieta
scialo da gran signore
rime ed inni d'amore.
Per sogni e per chimere
e per castelli in aria,
l'anima ho milionaria.
Talor dal mio forziere
ruban tutti i gioielli
due ladri: gli occhi belli.
V'entrar con voi pur ora,
ed i miei sogni usati
e i bei sogni miei
tosto si dileguar!
Ma il furto non m'accora
poichè, poichè v'ha preso stanza
la dolce speranza!
Or che mi conoscete,
parlate voi,
deh! parlate. Chi siete?
Vi piaccia dir!

MIMÌ

Sì.
Mi chiamano Mimì,
ma il mio nome è Lucia.
La storia mia è breve.
A tela o a seta ricamo in casa e fuori.
Son tranquilla e lieta
ed è mio svago far gigli e rose.
Mi piaccion quelle cose
che han sì dolce malìa,
che parlano d'amor, di primavere,
che parlano di sogni e di chimere,
quelle cose che han nome poesia.
Lei m'intende?

RODOLFO *(commosso)*

Sì.

MIMÌ

Mi chiamano Mimì,
il perchè non so.
Sola mi fo il pranzo da me stessa,
Non vado sempre a messa
ma prego assai il Signor.
Vivo sola, soletta,
là in una bianca cameretta:
guardo sui tetti e in cielo,

(si alza)

ma quando vien lo sgelo
il primo sole è mio.
Il primo baccio dell'aprile è mio!
il primo sole è mio!
Germoglia in un vaso una rosa . . .
Foglia a foglia la spio!
Così gentil il profumo d'un fior!
Ma i fior ch'io faccio, ahimè, non
        hanno odore!
Altro di me non le saprei narrare:
sono la sua vicina che la vien fuori
d'ora a importunare.

SCHAUNARD *(dal cortile)*

Ehi! Rodolfo!

COLLINE

Rodolfo!

MARCELLO

Olà. Non senti?
Lumaca!

MIMI

(*searches with her fingers*)

Nowhere?

RODOLFO

(*pretends to search but, guided by Mimi's voice and movements, tries to get near her*)

Nowhere!

MIMI

(*Mimi stoops to the floor, continuing to search for the key, at this moment Rodolfo reaches her and his hand encounters hers.*)

Ah!

RODOLFO

(*holding Mimi's hand*)

How cold your little hand is!
Let me warm it in my own.
Your key, don't mind it,
It's far too dark to find it.
A little later the moon will be rising,
And very soon then, the light will be stronger.
So stay a little longer,
And we'll talk a while together,
So you may know my vocation,
My ambitions.
Won't you?
I am, well who?
I am a poet. What am I doing?
Writing! How do I live then?
Somehow!
I have no worldly riches;
Ev'ry poetic measure
Holds a fabulous treasure.
In dreams and flights of fantasy
And castles in the air,
I am indeed a millionaire!
And now two eyes have stolen
Ev'ry priceless possession
Of my esteemed profession.
Their charming gentle glances
Captured my thoughts and visions,
And my daydreams and fancies
Swiftly as clouds depart.
However, I don't mind it.
Because they have suddenly brought me
New hope and revelation!
Now I feel that you know me,
So let me me ask you:
Won't you tell me who you are?
Please say you will!

MIMI

Yes.
I'm always called Mimi,
But my name is Lucia.
My story is a brief one:
I earn my living by sewing and embroidering.
Working gives me pleasure;
In leisure hours I make lilies and roses.
I dearly love those flowers,
They delight and enchant me,
They speak to me of love,
Of love and spring-time,
They speak to me of dreams and of illusions,
Of those wonders the world will call poetic.
You understand me?

RODOLFO (*moved*)

Yes.

MIMI

I'm always called Mimi,
I don't know just why!
Doing my work the daytime passes fairly,
I go to Mass but rarely,
Though ev'ry night I pray,
I live all by myself.
There from by lofty garret window
Over the roof-tops I see the sky.

(*She rises.*)

But, when the snow is thawing,
But, when the snow is thawing,
But, when the snow is thaw
Spring's first caress belongs to me,
The spring's first sunshine is mine!
When rosebuds are starting to blossom
Then I watch them unfolding.
How sweet the scene of a blooming flower!
But those I make myself,
Embroidered flowers, alas, they have no fragrance.
I'm afraid my life is not too exciting,
I am merely a neighbor who intruded
And interrupted your writing.

SCHAUNARD

(*from the court-yard*)

Eh! Rodolfo!

COLLINE

Rodolfo!

MARCELLO

Hello! Do you hear us?
You slow-poke!

COLLINE
Poetucolo!

SCHAUNARD
Accidenti al pigro!

RODOLFO (*alla finestra*)
Scrivo ancor tre righe a volo.

MIMÌ
(*avvicinandosi un poco alla finestra*)
Chi son?

RODOLFO
(*rivolgendosi a Mimì*)
Amici.

SCHAUNARD
Sentirai le tue.

MARCELLO
Che te ne fai lì solo?

RODOLFO
Non son solo. Siamo in due.
Andate da Momus, tenete il posto,
ci saremo tosto.

(*Rimane alla finestra, onde assicurarsi
che gli amici se ne vanno.*)

MARCELLO, SCHAUNARD, COLLINE
(*allontanandosi*)
Momus, Momus, Momus,
zitti e discreti andiamocene via.

SCHAUNARD, COLLINE
Momus, Momus,

MARCELLO
Trovò la poesia!

(*Mimì è ancora avvicinata alla finestra
per modo che i raggi lunari la illum-
inano: Rodolfo volgendosi scorge
Mimì avvolta come da un nimbo di
luce*)

RODOLFO
O soave fanciulla,
o dolce viso
di mite circonfuso alba lunar,
in te, ravviso
il sogno ch'io vorrei sempre sognar!
Fremon già nell'anima
le dolcezze estreme.
Fremon nell'anima
dolcezze estreme,
fremon dolcezze estreme,
nel baccio freme amor!

MIMÌ
Ah! tu sol comandi, amor!
tu sol comandi, amore!
Oh! come dolci scendono
le sue lusinghe al core . . .
tu sol comandi, amor!

(*Rodolfo la bacia.*)

MIMÌ (*svincolandosi*)
No, per pietà!

RODOLFO
Sei mia!

MIMÌ
V'aspettan gli amici

RODOLFO
Già mi mandi via?

MIMÌ (*titubante*)
Vorrei dir . . . ma non oso . . .

RODOLFO (*con gentilezza*)
Di'.

MIMÌ
(*con graziosa furberia*)
Se venissi con voi?

RODOLFO (*sopreso*)
Che? Mimì!
(*con intenzione tentatrice*)
Sarebbe cosi dolce restar qui.
C'è freddo fuori.

MIMÌ
(*con grande abbandono*)
Vi starò vicina!.

RODOLFO
E al ritorno? . . .

MIMÌ (*maliziosa*)
Curioso! . . .

RODOLFO
Dammi il braccio, mia piccina . . .

MIMÌ
(*da il braccio a Rodolfo*)
Obbedisco, signor!
(*S'avviano*)

RODOLFO
Che m'ami dì.

MIMÌ
Io t'amo!

RODOLFO E MIMÌ (*di fuori*)
Amor! Amor!
Amor!

COLLINE

What is keeping you?

SCHAUNARD

Are you writing a novel?

RODOLFO (*at the window*)

Three more lines and I'll be ready.

MIMI

(*approaching the window a little*)
Who's there?

RODOLFO (*turning to her*)

My colleagues.

SCHAUNARD

We will tell you plenty!

MARCELLO

Aren't you very lonely?

RODOLFO

I'm not lonely, someone's with me.
Why don't you go ahead,
Reserve a table, we will follow quickly.
(*Mimi goes still nearer the window.
The moonlight is falling upon her.*)

MARCELLO, SCHAUNARD, COLLINE

(*more and more in the distance*)
Momus, Momus, Momus
Now it is time we tactfully retired,

SCHAUNARD, COLLINE

Momus, Momus,

MARCELLO

The poet is inspired!

RODOLFO

(*Turning, Rodolfo sees Mimi with the
light like a halo around her.*)
O adorable angel,
O gentle vision,
Surrounded by the moonlight's silver
glow,
In your sweet person
I realize my fondest dreams of long ago!

RODOLFO

Never have I known before
So divine a rapture!
Radiant with happiness
My heart is glowing,
Now at last I have found you,
My one and only love!

MIMI

Ah! I've never known before,
A love so tender and glowing!
Oh, how its soothing power
Overcomes my heart with gladness,
How sweet to be in love!
(*Rodolfo kisses Mimi.*)

MIMI (*withdrawing*)

No, please don't.

RODOLFO

My sweetheart!

MIMI

Your friends are waiting . . .

RODOLFO

You're sending me away, then?

MIMI (*hesitating*)

I would say . . . but I dare not . . .

RODOLFO (*gently*)

What?

MIMI (*coquettishly*)

Would you take me along?

RODOLFO (*surprised*)

You, Mimi?
(*insinuatingly*)
Would you not rather stay at home with
me?
Out there it's freezing . . .

MIMI (*with great abandon*)

I'll stay close beside you!

RODOLFO

(*lovingly helps Mimi put on her shawl*)
And later?

MIMI (*archly*)

I wonder!

RODOLFO

Take my arm, my little darling.

MIMI

(*gives her arm to Rodolfo*)
I obey you, my lord!
(*They go arm in arm to the door.*)

RODOLFO

Your love is mine?

MIMI (*with abandon*)

I love you!

BOTH (*off-stage*)

My love, my love!
My love!

QUADRO II

AL QUARTIERE LATINO.

LA VIGILIA DI NATALE. *Un crocicchio di vie che al largo prende forma di piazzale; botteghe, venditori di ogni genere; da un lato il Caffè Momus.*

Nella folla si aggirano Rodolfo e Mimì. Colline presso alla botte di una rappezzatrice, Schaunard a una bottega di ferravecchi sta comperando una pipa e un corno, Marcello è spinto qua e là dal capriccio della gente. Gran folla e diversa; Borghesi, Soldati, Fantesche, Ragazzi, Bambine, Studenti, Sartine, Gendarmi, ecc. È sera. Le botteghe sono adorne di lampioncini e fanali accesi; un grande fanale illumina l' ingresso del Caffè Momus. Il Caffè è affollatissimo così che alcuni Borghesi sono costretti a sedere ad una tavola fuori all' aperto.

I VENDITORI

(sul limitare delle loro botteghe)

Aranci, datteri!
Caldi i marroni!
Ninnoli, croci! Torroni!
Panna montata!
Oh! la crostata!

Caramelle!
Fiori alle belle!
La crostata!
Panna montata!
Fringuelli, passeri!
Datteri!
Caldi marroni!
Panna, torroni!
Latte di cocco!
Oh! la crostata!
Panna montata!
Ninnoli, torroni!
Aranci, fiori!
Datteri, torroni!

Dal caffè.

(gridando e chiamando i camerieri)

Presto qua!
Camerier!
Un bicchier!
Corri!
Birra!
Da ber!

STUDENTI

Quanta folla! Che chiasso!

DONNE

Ah! Ah!

RAGAZZI

Aranci, ninnoli!
Caldi i marroni!
Caramelle! Tortoni!

DONNE

Quanta folla!

STUDENTI

Su, corriam!

DONNE

Stringiti a me, che chiasso!

STUDENTI

Stringiti a me. Su, corriam!

RAGAZZI

Su, corriamo, su, corriam!

DONNE E STUDENTI

Date il passo, corriam!
Quanta folla! su partiam!

RAGAZZI

Datteri, aranci! Latte di cocco!
Caldi i marroni!
Ninnoli, torroni!

DONNE E STUDENTI

Ah!

DONNE

Date il passo!
Ah! quanta folla!

DONNE E STUDENTI

Stringiti a me, corriam!

ACT II

The Latin Quarter

A square at the intersection of several streets: shops of all kinds; on one side, the Café Momus.

Christmas Eve

A milling crowd of various people: townspeople, soldiers, servants, children, boys and girls, students, working girls, gendarmes, etc. In front of their shops, vendors are shouting their wares. On one side, away from the crowd, Rodolfo and Mimi are strolling up and down. Colline is near the seamstress's shop: Schaunard is buying a pipe and horn at the ironmonger's; Marcello is caught up in the movements of the crowd. A group of townspeople are seated at an outside table in front of the Café Momus. It is evening. The shops are lit by little lamps: the street lights are also burning.

VENDORS

(in front of their shops)

Bananas, apricots!
Hot-roasted chestnuts!
Cabbages, carrots, tomatoes!
Pastry and fruitcake!
Say, what will you take?

(Rushing through the crowd and offering their different wares.)

Macaroni!
More for your money!
Lower prices!
Candies and ices!
Tobacco, licorice!
Necklaces!
Hot-roasted chestnuts!
Strawberry ices!
Coconut taffy!
Ginger and spices!
Coconut taffy!
Gingerbread and spices!
Oranges, apples!
Reasonable prices!

At Café Momus

GUESTS

(shouting and calling to the waiters)

Hurry up!

Let me pass!

Bring a glass!

Hurry!

Waiter!

A beer!

STUDENTS

Merry Christmas! Hello there!

WORKING GIRLS

Ah! Ah!

STREET URCHINS

Bananas, apricots!
Hot-roasted chestnuts!
Necklaces, carrots, potatoes!

GIRLS

What confusion!

STUDENTS

Come let's run!

GIRLS

Hold on to me, it's crowded!

STUDENTS

Hold on to me! This is fun!

URCHINS

Try and catch me, this is fun!

GIRLS AND STUDENTS

Look at the holiday crowd!
Let's go with them, come along!

URCHINS

Oranges, apples! Coconut slices!
Hot-roasted chestnuts!
Gingerbread and spices!

GIRLS AND STUDENTS

Ah!

GIRLS

Merry Christmas!
Ah, what an uproar!

GIRLS AND STUDENTS

Hold on to me, let's go!

Dal caffè

Dunque? Un caffè!

Da ber!

Camarier!

Olà!

VENDITORI

Latte di cocco!

Giubbe! Carote!

SCHAUNARD

(*Dopo aver soffiato nel corno che ha contrattato a lungo con un venditore di ferravecchi*)

Falso questo *Re*!

Falso questo *Re*!

Pipa corno quant'è? (*paga*)

(*Rodolfo e Mimì, a braccio, attraversano la folla avviati al negozio della modista.*)

COLLINE

(*presso la rappezzatrice che gli ha cucito la falda di un zimarrone*)

È un poco usato,

Ma è serio buon mercato . . .

RODOLFO

Andiam!

MIMÌ

Andiam per la cuffietta?

RODOLFO

Tienti al braccio stretta.

MIMÌ

A te mi stringo. Andiam!

RODOLFO

Andiam!

DUE MADRE

Emma, quando ti chiamo!

DONNE E STUDENTI

Che chiasso, stringiti a me!

STUDENTI

Quanta folla, su partiam!

RAGAZZI

Fringuelli e passeri, caldi i marron!

ALCUNI RAGAZZI

Voglio una lancia!

TUTTI RAGAZZI

Aranci, caldi i marron!

Datteri! ninnoli, aranci e fior!

MARCELLO

Io pur mi sento in vena di gridar:

Chi vuol, donnine allegre, un po'
d'amor?

(*avvicinandosi ad una ragazza*)

Facciamo insieme.

Facciamo a vendere e a comprar!

VENDITORI

Datteri! Trote!

UN VENDITORE AMBULANTE

(*attraversando la scena*)

Prugne di Tours!

MARCELLO

Io dò a un soldo il vergine mio cuor!

(*la ragazza si allontana ridendo*)

SCHAUNARD

(*armato della enorme pipa e del corno
da caccia*)

Fra spintoni e pestate accorrendo,

affretta la folla e si diletta

nel provar gioie matte—insoddisfatte.

DONNE

Ninnoli, spillete!

Datteri e caramelle!

RAGAZZI

Ah!

VENDITORI

Fiori alle belle!

GUESTS

Bring me a beer!

A beer!

And a glass!

Ho there!

VENDORS

Coconut-kisses,
Cabbage and carrots!

TWO MOTHERS

Emma! Come when I call you!

GIRLS AND STUDENTS

Be careful! Hold on to me!

STUDENTS

It's too noisy, come along!

URCHINS

Pastry and chocolate, Turkish delight!

SOME URCHINS

I want some candy!

ALL URCHINS

A bag of hot-roasted nuts!
Oranges, necklaces, flowers and nuts!

SCHAUNARD

(*After blowing the horn several times,
he tries to strike a bargain with the
iron-monger.*)

Listen to this E!
It is out of key!
You can take it from me!

(*He pays the bill.*)

(*Rodolfo and Mimi, arm in arm, push
their way through the crowd to get
near the hat shop.*)

COLLINE

(*to the seamstress, who has been mend-
ing the hem of his coat*)

A trifle shiny, but old and very worthy.

(*pays, then carefully distributes the
books in the many pockets of his
coat*)

(*Marcello all alone in the crowd, a
bundle under his arm, eyeing the girls
who brush past him.*)

RODOLFO

Let's go! . . .

MIMI

To buy a pretty bonnet?

RODOLFO

Stay close to me, my darling.

MIMI

I'm right beside you. Let's go.

RODOLFO

Let's go.

(*They enter the hat shop.*)

MARCELLO

Among so many young and lovely girls
There surely must be one or two left
   for me!

(*approaching a young girl*)

You, too, look lonely.
I think we'd make a handsome pair!

VENDORS

Oranges!
Lobster!

STROLLING VENDOR

(*crossing the stage*)

Hot lemonade!

MARCELLO

That you should come with me is only
   fair!

(*The young girl runs away, laughing.*)

SCHAUNARD

(*armed with his huge pipe and hunting
horn*)

I can never see why people crowd
   like herds of cattle
In all this noise and prattle,
How they find satisfaction
In such distraction!

SALESGIRLS

Souvenirs and laces!
Caramels and choc'late kisses!

URCHINS

Ah!

VENDORS

Flow'rs for the misses!

COLLINE
(*se ne viene al ritrovo, agitando trionfalmente un vecchio libro*)
Copia rara, anzi unica:
la grammatica Runica!

SCHAUNARD
Uomo onesto! . . .

MARCELLO
(*arriva al Caffè Momus e vi trova
Schaunard e Colline*)
A cena!

SCHAUNARD, COLLINE
Rodolfo!

MARCELLO
Entrò da una modista.
(*Rodolfo e Mimì escono dalla bottega*)

RODOLFO
Vieni, gli amici aspettano.

MIMÌ
Mi sta ben questa cuffietta rosa?

VENDITORI
Panna montata!

RAGAZZI
Latte di cocco!

BORGHESI
Facciam coda alla gente!
Raggaze, state attente!
Che chiasso! Quanta folla!

Pigliam via Mazzarino!
Io soffoco, partiamo!
Vedi, il caffè e vicin!
Andiam, là da Momus!

RODOLFO
Chi guardi? . . .

MIMÌ
Sei geloso?

RODOLFO
All' uom felice sta il sospetto accanto.

MIMÌ
Sei felice?

RODOLFO
Ah! sì, tanto. E tu?

MIMÌ
Sì, tanto.

DONNE, STUDENTI
Là da Momus!
Andiam!
Andiam!
(*Mimì e Rodolfo raggiungono gli
amici.*)

VENDITORI
Oh! la crostata!
Panna montata!

LA FOLLA (*dal Caffè*)
Camerier!
Un bicchier!
Presto, olà!
Ratafià!

RODOLFO
Sei bruna e quel color ti dona.

MIMÌ
(*guardando con rimpianto verso la
bottega della modista*)
Bel vezzo di corallo!

RODOLFO
Ho uno zio milionario
Se fa senno il buon Dio
voglio comprarti un vezzo assai più bel.

RAGAZZI
Ha! ha! ha! ha! ha! ha! ha! ha!
ha! ha!

DONNE, STUDENTI
Ha, ha!

RAGAZZI, DONNE, STUDENTI
Ha! ha! ha! ha! ha! ha!

VENDITORI
Oh! la crostata!

RAGAZZI
Oh! la crostata!

VENDITORI
Panna montata!
Aranci, datteri, ninnoli, fior!
Fringuelli, passeri, panna, torron!

COLLINE
Odio il profano volgo al par
d'Orazio.

SCHAUNARD
Ed io quando mi sazio
vo' abbondanza di spazio.

MARCELLO (*al cameriere*)
Vogliamo una cena prelibata.
Lesto!

SCHAUNARD
Per molti!

MARCELLO, SCHAUNARD,
COLLINE (*al cameriere*)
Lesto!

COLLINE
(*triumphantly waving in his hand a rare book*)
This rare book is the theory
Of an ancient philosophy!

SCHAUNARD
Quite a bargain!

MARCELLO
(*shouts to Colline and Schaunard*)
To dinner!

SCHAUNARD AND COLLINE
Rodolfo!

MARCELLO
He went into that hat-shop!

RODOLFO
(*leaving the hat-shop together with Mimi*)
Come, dear, our friends are waiting there.

MIMI
Do you think this bonnet is becoming?

VENDORS
Strawberry ices!

URCHINS
Coconut slices!

VENDORS
Gingerbread spices!
Strawberry ices!

CITIZENS (*from the café*)
Waiter here!
One more beer!
Hurry up!
Aquavit!

RODOLFO
In anything you would look lovely!

MIMI
(*looking admiringly at the window display of a shop*)
Oh, what a lovely bracelet!

RODOLFO
My old uncle who has millions
Soon will leave for greener pastures.
Then I shall buy you twenty strings of pearls!

URCHINS
Ha! ha! ha! ha! ha! ha! ha! ha! ha! ha!

GIRLS AND STUDENTS
Ha! ha!

URCHINS, GIRLS AND STUDENTS
Ha! ha! ha! ha! ha! ha!

TOWNSPEOPLE
Let's see where they are going!
Look how the crowd is growing!
How noisy! What an uproar!
(*moving towards Rue Mazarin*)
They're turning around the corner!
They're tearing me to pieces!
Let's try Café Momus!
All right, Café Momus!
(*They enter the café.*)

RODOLFO
You're flirting?

MIMI
Are you jealous?

RODOLFO
A man in love is bound to be suspicious.

MIMI
Do you love me?

RODOLFO
Ah, forever!
And you?

MIMI
I love you!

GIRLS AND STUDENTS
There is Momus!
Go in!
Go in!

VENDORS
Coconut slices!

URCHINS
Coconut slices!

VENDORS
Gingerbread spices!

URCHINS
Gingerbread spices!

VENDORS
Flow'rs for the ladies!

URCHINS
Oranges, apples, and hot-roasted nuts!

VENDORS
Oranges, apricots, ginger and spice
Pastry and chocolate, Turkish delight!

COLLINE
I cannot stand a vulgar crowd of people.

SCHAUNARD
And I, when I am dining,
Must have room for reclining.

MARCELLO (*to the waiter*)
We must have a very special supper!
Hurry!

SCHAUNARD
And plenty!

MARCELLO, SCHAUNARD, COLLINE
(*to the waiter*)
Hurry!

PARPIGNOL (*da lontano*)
Ecco i giocattoli di Parpignol!

RODOLFO
(*giungendo con Mimì*)
Due posti.

COLLINE
Finalmente!

RODOLFO
Eccoci qui.
Questa è Mimì gaia fioraia.
Il suo venir completa la bella
    compagnia,
perchè son io il poeta,
    essa la poesia.
Dal mio cervel sbocciano i canti
    dalle sue dita sbocciano i fior
    dall' anime esultanti sboccia l'amor!

MARCELLO, SCHAUNARD, COLLINE
Ah, ah, ah, ah!

MARCELLO (*ironico*)
Dio, che concetti rari!

COLLINE
Digna est intrari.

SCHAUNARD
Ingrediat si necessit.

COLLINE
Io non dò che un: *accessit.*
(*Rodolfo fa sedere Mimì; seggono tutti;
il cameriere ritorna presentando la
lista delle vivande.*)

PARPIGNOL
(*da lontano, avvicinandosi*)
Ecco i giocattoli di Parpignol!

COLLINE
(*con enfasi romantica al cameriere*)
Salame . . .
(*Da via Delfino sbocca un carretto tutto
a fronzoli e fiori, illuminato a pallon-
cini; chi lo spinge è Parpignol.*)

RAGGAZZI, BAMBINE
Parpignol, Parpignol!

RAGAZZI E BAMBINE
(*circondano il carretto, saltellando*)
Ecco Parpignol! Parpignol! Parpignol!
Col carretto tutto fior!
Ecco Parpignol!
Parpignol! Parpignol! Parpignol!
Voglio la tromba, il cavallin,
Il tambur, tamburel,
Voglio il cannon, voglio il frustin.
Dei soldati i drappel.

SCHAUNARD
Cervo arrosto!

MARCELLO
(*esaminando la carta*)
Un tacchino!

SCHAUNARD
Vin del Reno!

COLLINE
Vin da tavola!

SCHAUNARD
Aragosta senza crosta!

MAMME
(*strillanti e minaccianti*)
Ah! razza di furfanti indemoniati,
che ci venite a fare in questo loco?
A casa, a letto! Via brutti sguaiati,
gli scappellotti vi parranno poco!
A casa, a letto, razza di furfanti, a letto!
(*Una mamma prende per un orecchio
un ragazzo*)

RAGAZZO (*piagnucolando*)
Vo' la tromba, il cavallin.

RODOLFO
E tu Mimì, che vuoi!

MIMÌ
La crêma.
(*Le mamme, intenerite, si decidono a
comperare da Parpignol: i ragazzi
saltano di gioia*)

SCHAUNARD
(*con somma importanza al cameriere*)
E gran sfarbo. C'è una dama!

(*Rodolfo and Mimi come into the Café Momus.*)

PARPIGNOL (*from a distance*)
Come, buy some Christmas toys from Parpignol!

RODOLFO
Two places!
(*meets his friends and presents Mimi to them*)

COLLINE
Here's our poet!

RODOLFO
Yes, here we are.
This is Mimi, she is an artist.
With her our chosen circle
Now at last is completed,
You see, although I am the poet,
She is the purest poetry!
Here in my mind blossom the verses,
And from her fingers blossom the flow'rs,
Two joyous hearts united
Blossom in love, blossom in love!

MARCELLO, SCHAUNARD, COLLINE
Ha! Ha! Ha! Ha!

MARCELLO (*ironically*)
That was a flow'ry oration!

COLLINE
Worthy presentation!

SCHAUNARD
She passes my inspection!

COLLINE
Then I make no objection!
(*They all take their places at the table, as the waiter returns.*)

PARPIGNOL (*now much nearer*)
Come, buy your Christmas toys from Parpignol!

COLLINE
(*seeing the waiter, he shouts loudly*)
Salami!

(*From the Rue Dauphin a cart is seen, all decorated with greens and flowers, and lit by Chinese lanterns: pushing the cart is Parpignol.*)

CHILDREN (*off-stage*)
Parpignol, Parpignol!

CHILDREN (*entering*)
Follow Parpignol, Parpignol, Parpignol!
With his cart all filled with toys!
Follow Parpignol,
Parpignol, Parpignol, Parpignol!
I want a trumpet and a ball!
Buy a nice little ship!
I want a carriage and a doll!
Buy a horse and a whip!

SCHAUNARD
Mushroom omelet!

MARCELLO
(*studying the menu*)
Roasted capon!

SCHAUNARD
I want Rhine-wine!

COLLINE
Sparkling Burgundy!

SCHAUNARD
And a casserole of lobster!

THE MOTHERS
(*shrieking and threatening*)
You naughty children are an awful bother!
Why don't you stop your fighting and your shouting!
Go home at once, or I will tell your father,
And he will give you all a thorough clouting!
Go home now, you naughty pack of little rascals!
It's bed-time!
(*One mother takes her little boy by the ear.*)

A BOY
Want a trumpet and a horse!
(*whimpering*)

RODOLFO
And you Mimi, you wish?

MIMI
Some pastry!
(*The mothers, relenting, decide to buy from Parpignol: the children jump for joy.*)

SCHAUNARD
(*with an air of great importance to the waiter*)
Bring the best one, for the lady!

(*Parpignol prende giù per via Vecchia Commedia: i ragazzi e le bambine allegramente lo seguono marciando e fingendo suonare gli strumenti infantili acquistatigli.*)

RAGAZZI

Viva Parpignol, Parpignol!
Il tambur, tamburel!
dei soldati, il drappel!

MARCELLO

(*come continuando il discorso*)

Signorina Mimì, che dono raro le ha fatto il suo Rodolfo?

MIMÌ

Una cuffietta a pizzi tutta
rosa ricamata.
Coi miei cappelli bruni ben si fonde.
Da tanto tempo tal cuffietta
è cosa desiata.
Ed egli ha letto quel che il core asconde.
Ora colui che legge dentro a un cuore.
Sa l'amore ed è lettore.

SCHAUNARD

Esperto professore!

COLLINE

Che ha già diplomi e
Non son armi prime
Le sue rime.

SCHAUNARD

Tanto che sembra ver
Ciò ch'egli esprime.

MARCELLO

O bella età d'inganni e d'utopie!
Si crede, spera e tutto bello appare.

RODOLFO

La più divina delle poesie
è quella, amico, che c'insegna amare!

MIMÌ

Amare è dolce ancora più del miele!
Più del miele!

MARCELLO (*stizzito*)

Secondo il palato
è miele o fiele!

MIMÌ (*sorpresa a Rodolfo*)

O Dio, l'ho offeso!

RODOLFO

È in lutto, o mia Mimì.

SCHAUNARD, COLLINE

Allegri e un toast!

MARCELLO (*al cameriere*)

Qua del liquor!

MIMÌ, RODOLFO, MARCELLO

E via i pensier,
alti i bicchier!
Beviam!

TUTTI

Beviam!

MARCELLO

(*che da lontano ha veduto Musetta, interrompe gridando*)

Ch'io beva del tossico! Essa!

(*si lascia cadere sulla sedia*)

(*All' angolo di via Mazzarino appare una bellissima signora, dal fare civettuolo e allegro, dal sorriso provocante. Le vien dietro un vecchio pomposo e lezioso.*)

RODOLFO, SCHAUNARD, COLLINE

(*con sorpresa vedendo Musetta*)

Oh! Musetta!

BOTTEGAIE

To'! Lei! Sì!
To'! Lei! Musetta!
Siamo in auge!
Che toeletta!

ALCINDORO (*trafelato*)

Come un facchino . . .
Correr di qua . . . di là . . .
No! no! non ci stà! . . .

MUSETTA

(*con passi rapidi, guardando qua e là come in cerca di qualcuno mentre Alcindoro la segue, sbuffando e stizzito*)

Vien, Lulù! Vien, Lulù!

ALCINDORO

Non ne posso più . . .
non ne posso più!

(*la bella signora senza curarsi di lui si avvia verso il Caffè Momus e prende posto alla tavola lasciata libera*)

(*Parpignol starts down the Rue Vielle Comédie: the boys and girls follow him gaily, marching, and pretending to play their new toy instruments.*)

CHILDREN

Follow Parpignol, Parpignol!
Tarata, taratam!
Dadadum, dadadum!

MARCELLO
(*continuing their conversation*)

May I ask, Miss Mimi, what special present
Has your Rodolfo bought you?

MIMI

He bought me a delightful little
    hand-embroidered bonnet.
Against my hair its shade is so
    becoming.
As long as I remember
I had set my heart upon it.
He read my mind without my even
    saying.
A man who reads the heart's concealed
    ambition
Is no novice,
He knows what love is!

SCHAUNARD

A clever definition!

COLLINE

He has experience,
And for years rehearses,
Writing verses!

SCHAUNARD

All that he says sounds true
As he converses.

MARCELLO

O lovely state of dreams and
    admiration!
You hope, believe, and see the world in
    sunshine.

RODOLFO

The most divine of poet's inspiration
Is that, my friend, which teaches us to
    love!

MIMI

To be in love is very close to heaven,
Close to heaven!

MARCELLO (*angrily*)

For some it is heaven,
For others, damnation!

MIMI (*surprised, to Rodolfo*)

O dear, did I hurt him?

RODOLFO

He mourns his former love.

SCHAUNARD AND COLLINE

It's time for a toast!

MARCELLO (*to the waiter*)

Fill up my glass!

MIMI, RODOLFO, MARCELLO

Down with despair!
Life is so fair!
A toast!

ALL FIVE

A toast!

MARCELLO

(*stops, having seen Musetta approaching*) (*shouting*)

Bring me a dose of arsenic! She's here!
    (*He slumps down in his chair.*)
(*From the corner of the Rue Mazarin a beautiful young lady enters, a gay coquette with a provocative smile. She is accompanied by a pompous old man, pretentious both in a manner and in dress.*)

RODOLFO, SCHAUNARD, COLLINE
(*surprised, seeing Musetta*)

Look! Musetta!

SHOP WOMEN

Look! Where? There!
What? She! Musetta!
Bold as ever!
To the letter!

ALCINDORO (*out of breath*)

Just like a porter . . .
Running around like mad . . .
No no! not for me!

(*Musetta enters, followed by Alcindoro, peevishly huffing and panting.*)

MUSETTA (*as if calling her puppy*)

Come, Fifi! Come, Fifi!

ALCINDORO

It's too much for me!
It's too much for me!

(*Musetta sees the table where the friends are sitting outside the Café Momus, and signals Alcindoro to reserve the table which the townspeople have just left.*)

SCHAUNARD
Quel brutto coso mi par che sudi!

ALCINDORO
Come! qui fuori? qui?

MUSETTA
Siedi Lulù.
(*Alcindoro siede irritato, rialzando il bavero del pastrano.*)

ALCINDORO
Tali nomignoli prego
serbateli al tu per tu!
(*Un cameriere s' è avvicinato premuroso e prepara la tavola.*)

MUSETTA
Non farmi il Barbablù!
(*siede anch'essa al tavolo, rivolta verso il Caffè*)

COLLINE
(*esaminando il vecchio*)
È il vizio contegnoso . . .

MARCELLO
Colla casta Susanna.

MIMÌ (*a Rodolfo*)
È pur ben vestita.

RODOLFO
Gli angeli vanno nudi.

MIMÌ
La conosci! Chi è?

MARCELLO
Domandatelo a me.
Il suo nome: Musetta;
cognome: Tentazione!
Per sua vocazione
fa la rosa dei venti;
gira e muta soventi
d' amanti e d' amore
E come la civetta,
è uccello sanguinario;
il suo cibo ordinario
è il cuore . . .
Mangia il cuore! . . .
Per questo io non ne ho più . . .
Passatemi il ragù!

MUSETTA
(Marcello mi vide . . .
e non mi guarda il vile!
Quel Schaunard che ride!
Mi fan tutti una bile!
Se potessi picchiar!
Se potessi graffiar!

Ma non ho sotto man
che questo pellican.
Aspetta!)
Ehi! Camerier!
(*Musetta annusando un piatto*)
Cameriere! Questo piatto
ha una puzza di rifritto!
(*Getta il piatto; il cameriere si affretta a raccogliere i cocci.*)

ALCINDORO
No. Musetta . . . zitto, zitto!

MUSETTA
(*rabbiosa, sempre guardando Marcello*)
(Non si volta.)

ALCINDORO
No. Musetta . . .
zitto, zitto!

MUSETTA
(Ah non si volta!)

ALCINDORO
A chi parli?

MUSETTA (*rabbiosa*)
(Ora lo batto, lo batto!)

ALCINDORO
Con chi parli?

COLLINE
Questo pollo e un poema!

SCHAUNARD
Il vino è prelibato.

MUSETTA (*seccata*)
Al cameriere!
Non seccar!
Voglio fare il mio piacere.

ALCINDORO
Parla pian, parla pian!

MUSETTA
Vo' far quel che mi pare!
Non seccar!

DONNE
Guarda, guarda chi si vede,
proprio lei, Musetta!

STUDENTI
Con quel vecchio che balbetta.

SCHAUNARD
Now the old codger will start to suffer!

ALCINDORO
Sit here? In the open? No!

MUSETTA
Stop it, Fifi!
(*Alcindoro, testy and irritated, sits down, and turns up his coat collar.*)

ALCINDORO (*grumbling*)
Please do not use any pet-names
In public when talking to me!
(*A waiter enters and sets the table.*)

MUSETTA
Don't take that tone with me!
(*Sits down at the table, facing the café.*)

COLLINE
(*scrutinizing the old man*)
A dangerous seducer!

MARCELLO
With his chaste little pigeon!

MIMI (*to Rodolfo*)
But her dress is lovely!

RODOLFO
Angels must do without them.

MIMI (*with curiosity*)
Do you know who she is?

MARCELLO
Let me answer you this.
Her first name is Musetta.
Her last one is Temptation!
By way of vocation,
Like a reed in the breezes,
She will change in her love
And her lovers very often,
Exactly like the raven,
She's callous and malicious,
And her fav'rite of dishes
Is heart-blood!
Ravenous prey-bird!
And she ate my heart, too!
Please pass me the ragout!

MUSETTA
(Marcello has seen me,
But he ignores me, the scoundrel!
That Schaunard is laughing!
One's as bad as the other!
I would blacken their eyes!
If I just had a chance!

And I am here alone
With this ridiculous dunce!
I'll show you!)
Hey! waiter here!

(*sniffing at her plate*)
The smell of this plate is too distasteful!
(*Throws the plate to the ground. The waiter picks up the pieces.*)

ALCINDORO
Stop! Musetta!
Don't be wasteful!

MUSETTA
(*seeing that Marcello has not turned around*)
(He's not looking!)

ALCINDORO
Quiet, quiet, quiet!
Hold your temper!

MUSETTA
(Still he ignores me!)

ALCINDORO
What's the trouble?

MUSETTA (*furious*)
(If I could tear him to pieces!)

ALCINDORO
What's the trouble?

COLLINE
The soufflé is delicious!

SCHAUNARD
The wine is simply perfect!

MUSETTA
This stupid waiter! (*annoyed*)
That's enough!
I'll do just what I feel like doing!

ALCINDORO
Not so loud! Not so loud!

MUSETTA
I don't need you to tell me!
And I want to be left alone!

WORKING GIRLS
Look who's here on exhibition,
Mad'moiselle Musetta!

STUDENTS
What a priceless proposition!

DONNE, STUDENTI

Proprio lei, Musetta!
Ah, ah, ah, ah, ah, ah, ah!

MUSETTA

(Che sia geloso di questa mummia?
Vediam se mi resta tanto poter
su lui da farlo cedere!)

ALCINDORO

La convenienza . . . il grado . . .
la virtù . . .

SCHAUNARD

La commedia è stupenda!

MUSETTA

(*guardando Marcello*)
Tu non mi guardi!

ALCINDORO

(*credendo rivolte a lui queste parole*)
Vedi bene che ordino!

SCHAUNARD

La commedia è stupenda!

COLLINE

Stupenda!

RODOLFO (*a Mimì*)

Sappi per tuo
governo che non darei
perdono in sempiterno.

SCHAUNARD

Essa all'un parla
perchè l'altro intenda.

MIMÌ

Io t'amo tanto,
e sono tutta tua!
Che mi parli di perdono?

COLLINE (*a Schaunard*)

E l'altro invan crudel,
finge di non capir, ma sugge miel!

MUSETTA

Ma il tuo cuore martella.

ALCINDORO

Parla piano!

MUSETTA

(*Civettuola, volgendosi con intenzione
a Marcello il quale comincia ad
agitarsi.*)

Quando me'n vo',
quando me'n vo soletta per la via
la gente sosta e mira,
e la bellezza mia
tutta ricerca in me
ricerca in me da capo a piè.

MARCELLO

Legatemi alla seggiola!

ALCINDORO

Quella gente che dirà?

MUSETTA

Ed assaporo allor
la bramosia sottil,
che da gl'occhi traspira
e dai palesi vezzi intender sa
alle occulte beltà.

(*alzandosi*)

Così l'effluvio del desio
tutta m'aggira
felice mi fa!

E tu che sai
che memori e ti struggi,
da me tanto rifuggi?
So ben: le angoscie tue non le vuoi dir,
non le vuoi dir, so ben
ma ti senti morir!

ALCINDORO

(*si avvicina a Musetta*)

Quel canto scurrile
mi muove la bile!

MIMÌ (*a Rodolfo*)

Io vedo ben
che quella poveretta,
tutta invaghita ell'è!
Tutta invaghita di Marcel,
tutta invaghita ell'è!

ALCINDORO

Quella gente che dirà?

RODOLFO (*a Mimì*)

Marcello un dì l'amò.
La fraschetta l'abbandonò,
per poi darsi a miglior vita!

SCHAUNARD

Ah! Marcello cederà!

BOTH GROUPS

That's just like Musetta!
Ha ha ha ha ha ha ha!

MUSETTA

(Could he be jealous of such a
mummy?
Let's see if my power over his heart
Is strong enough to make him yield!)

ALCINDORO

Your reputation . . . your virtue.
My good name!

SCHAUNARD

This is simply stupendous!

MUSETTA (*facing Marcello*)

You still ignore me!

ALCINDORO

(*believing that Musetta had meant
him*)
Don't you see I am ordering?

SCHAUNARD

It is stimply stupendous!

COLLINE

Stupendous!

RODOLFO (*to Mimi*)

If you should ever
Treat me like that I never,
Never would forgive you!

SCHAUNARD

She speaks to one
And knows the other listens.

MIMI

Darling, I love you
For now and ever after!
So why talk about forgiving?

COLLINE (*to Schaunard*)

The other one pretends
But he's a piece of putty in her hands!

MUSETTA

But your heart throbs and hammers,

ALCINDORO

Softer, softer!

MUSETTA

(*still seated, and obviously directing her
attentions to Marcello, who is beginning to feel uneasy*)

Day after day
When I am strolling by on promenade,
The people turn admiringly,
Praising my dazzling beauty,
With eager eyes they gaze,
They gaze at me
Wherever I go!

MARCELLO

Will someone please hold on to me?

ALCINDORO

(*on pins and needles*)
What will people think of you?

MUSETTA

And then I savor keenly
That intense desire,
Which is burning in their glances,
And proudly show my ravishing attire,
With enchanting appeal.
(*rising*)
And when the wave of fervent longing
Invites romances,

How happy I feel,
How happy I feel!
You must remember,
Your passion still must burn for me,
Why do you not return to me?
I know, you fight your tortured heart
in vain,
You fight your heart in vain,
For you love me again!

ALCINDORO

(*coming closer to Musetta*)
This meaningless ditty
Begins to annoy me!
Begins to annoy me!

MIMI (*to Rodolfo*)

It's plain to see
The beautiful Musetta
Adores your friend Marcel,
She is in love with your Marcel,
Head over heels in love!

ALCINDORO

What will people think of you?

RODOLFO (*to Mimi*)

She loved him once, you know,
But one day she let him go,
Went in search for something better.

SCHAUNARD

Ah, Marcello soon will bow!

COLLINE

Chi sa mai quel che avverrà!

SCHAUNARD

(Trovan dolce al pari il laccio
chi lo tende e chi ci dà.)

COLLINE

Santi numi, in simil briga
mai Colline intopperà!

MUSETTA

(Ah! Marcello smania,
Marcello è vinto!)

ALCINDORO

Parla pian! Zitta, zitta!

MIMÌ

(Quell' infelice mi muove a pietà!)

(a Rodolfo)

T'amo!

RODOLFO

Mimì!

COLLINE

Essa è bella io non son cieco!

SCHAUNARD

(Quel bravaccio a momenti cederà!)
Stupenda è la commedia!

MUSETTA

So ben, le angoscie tue non le vuoi dir,
ah! ma ti senti morir.
Io voglio fare il mio piacere!
Voglio far quel che mi par, non seccar,
non seccar, non seccar!

MIMÌ

Quell' infelice mi muove a pietà!
l'amor ingeneroso è tristo amor!
Quell' infelice,
ah! ah! mi muove, mi muove a pietà!

RODOLFO

È fiacco amor quel che le offese
vendicar non sa!
Non risorge spento amor!
È fiacco amore, quel che le offese
vendicar non sa!

SCHAUNARD (a Colline)

Marcello cederà!
Se tal vaga persona, ti trattasse a tu
per tu,

Ia tua scienza brontolona manderesti
a Belzebù!

COLLINE

Ma piaccionmi assai più una pipa e un
testo greco!
mi piaccion assai più!
Essa è bella, non son cieco,
ma piaccionmi assai più una pipa e un
testo greco!

ALCINDORO

Modi, garbo!
Zitta, zitta!

MUSETTA

(Or convien liberarsi del vecchio!)
(fingendo provare un vivo dolore)
Ahi! qual dolore, qual bruciore!

ALCINDORO

Che c'è? Dove?

MUSETTA

Al piè!

ALCINDORO

(abbassandosi per slacciare la scarpa a
Musetta)

MARCELLO

(commosso sommamente)

Gioventù mia,
tu non sei morta
nè di te morto è il sovvenir!
Se tu battessi alla mia porta
t'andrebbe il mio core ad aprir,
ad aprir!

MUSETTA

Sciogli, slaccia!
rompi, straccia!
Te ne imploro . . .
Laggiù c'è un calzolaio!
Corri, presto!
Ne voglio un altro paio.
Ahi! che fitta,
maledetta scarpa stretta!
Or la levo!

(Si leva la scarpa e la mette sulla
tavola)

Eccola qua!
Corri, va, corri!
Presto, va! va!

ALCINDORO

Imprudente!
Quella gente che dirà?
Ma il mio grado! Vuoi ch'io com-
prometta?
Aspetta! Musetta! Vo'!

(Disperato, prende la scarpa e rapid-
amente se la caccia nel panciotto,
e si abbottona maestoso l'abito.)

COLLINE

Anything may happen now!

SCHAUNARD

(Both the victor and the victim
Seem to like the parts they play.)

COLLINE

From the clutches of a woman
I, Colline, must keep away!

MUSETTA

(Ah! Marcello loves me,
Marcello will surrender!)

ALCINDORO

Not so loud! Softly, softly!

MIMI

(I do feel sorry for that unhappy girl!)

(to Rodolfo)

Darling!

RODOLFO

Mimi!

COLLINE

There's no doubt that she is pretty!

SCHAUNARD

Now it won't be long until he will give
in!
The game is most exciting!

MUSETTA

And yet your anguished heart you fight
in vain!
Ah! and you love me again!
I'll do just what I feel like doing!
I'll do only what I like, let me go!
Let me go, let me go!

MIMI

I do feel sorry for that most unhappy
girl!
A selfish love is a dreary affair!
It makes me feel sad,
Ah, what a pity, a pity and a shame!

RODOLFO

It is a miserable love that won't defend
itself!
You can't revive a love that is dead!
It is a stale love, gone is all its
brilliance,
And its burning flame!

SCHAUNARD *(to Colline)*

Marcello won't resist!
If such a lovely lady should ever cast
her eyes on you,

You would burn your books on science,
and behave as others do!

COLLINE

But I prefer my pipe and my comfort-
able slippers,
And Greek philosophers!
There's no doubt that she is pretty,
But I prefer my pipe and my comfort-
able slippers!

ALCINDORO

Manners, manners!
Quiet, quiet!

MUSETTA

(Now it's time to get rid of my pet
here!)
*(pretending to feel a terrible pain in
her foot)*
Ow! this is awful, it will kill me!

ALCINDORO

What now? What's wrong?

MUSETTA

My foot!
*(Alcindoro stoops down to untie
Musetta's shoe.)*

MARCELLO *(deeply moved)*

Lovely Musetta,
How could I have forgotten,
I find myself in love again!
No matter what has come between us,
My heart is forever yours alone,
Yours alone!

MUSETTA

Slash the laces!
Rip the leather!
Strip the shoe off!
Nearby there is a shoe-store,
Hurry, quickly!
And get another pair.
It drives me crazy!
Off it comes!
*(takes off the shoe and puts it on the
table)*
So there you are!
Hurry, go quickly!
Hurry on! Go!

ALCINDORO

What impudence!
What will all the people say?
My position! You provoke a scandal!
How dare you? Musetta! No!
*(quickly hides Musetta's shoes under
his coat, runs off-stage, quickly)*

SCHAUNARD, COLLINE
La commedia è stupenda!

MUSETTA
Marcello!

MARCELLO
Sirena!

(*Musetta si alza e si getta nelle braccia di Marcello, che non sa più resistere.*)

SCHAUNARD
Siamo all' ultima scena!

(*Un cameriere porta il conto.*)

RODOLFO, SCHAUNARD, COLLINE
Il conto!

SCHAUNARD
Così presto?

(*Tamburi lontanissimi sulla scena*)

COLLINE
Chi l' ha richiesto?

SCHAUNARD
Vediam!

(*Lontanissima si ode la ritirata militare, che poco a poco va avvicinandosi*)

RODOLFO, COLLINE
(*osservando il conto*)
Caro!

RODOLFO, SCHAUNARD, COLLINE
(*tastandosi le tasche vuote*)
Fuori il danaro!

SCHAUNARD
Colline, Rodolfo e tu Marcel?

RAGAZZI
La Ritirata!

MARCELLO
Siamo all' asciutto!

SCHAUNARD
Come?

RODOLFO
Ho trenta soldi in tutto!

DONNE, STUDENTI
La Ritirata!

BORGHESI
(*Accorrendo da sinistra—la ritirata essendo ancor lontana, la gente corre da un lato all' altro della scena, guardando da quale via si avanzano i militari.*)
La Ritirata!

MARCELLO, SCHAUNARD, COLLINE
Come? Non ce n'è più?

SCHAUNARD
Ma il mio tesoro ov'è!

(*Portano le mani alle tasche: sono vuote: nessuno sa spiegarsi la rapida scomparsa degli scudi di Schaunard; sorpresi si guardano l' un l' altro.*)

RAGAZZI
S'avvicinan per di qua?

MUSETTA (*al cameriere*)
Il mio conto date a me.

DONNE, STUDENTI
No! di là!

RAGAZZI
S'avvicinan per di là!

DONNE, STUDENTI
Vien di qua!

(*Mamme e fanciulle alle finestre ed ai balconi guardando la ritirata che arriva.*)

RAGAZZI
No! vien di là!

MUSETTA
(*al cameriere che lo consegna*)
Bene!

VENDITORI, BORGHESI
Largo! largo!

RAGAZZI
Voglio veder!
voglio sentir!

MUSETTA
Presto sommate quello con questo!

MAMME
Lisetta, vuoi tacer!
Tonio, la vuoi finir!

SCHAUNARD AND COLLINE
The performance is amazing!

MUSETTA
Marcello!

MARCELLO
Musetta!
(*Musetta and Marcello embrace each other passionately.*)

SCHAUNARD
Now the drama is ending!
(*A waiter brings in the bill.*)

RODOLFO, SCHAUNARD, COLLINE
The bill?

SCHAUNARD
Not already?
(*Drums are heard in the distance off-stage*)

COLLINE
Did someone ask for it?

SCHAUNARD (*to the waiter*)
Let's see!
(*The Tattoo, first heard from a great distance, is gradually getting louder as the soldiers approach.*)

RODOLFO AND COLLINE
(*studying the bill*)
Expensive!

RODOLFO, SCHAUNARD, COLLINE
(*emptying their pockets*)
Empty your pockets!

SCHAUNARD
Rodolfo, Marcel, and you Colline?

STREET URCHINS
(*running on-stage*)
There are the bugles!

MARCELLO
We are insolvent!

SCHAUNARD
Really?

RODOLFO
I haven't got a penny!

GIRLS, STUDENTS
There are the bugles!

TOWNS-PEOPLE
(*Running on-stage from the left, the Tattoo is still quite a distance away, and the people run in from all directions, looking about to see from which road the soldiers will enter.*)
There are the bugles!

MARCELLO, SCHAUNARD, COLLINE
Really! Nothing at all?

SCHAUNARD
Has someone seen my purse?
(*They turn their pockets inside out: they are empty: no one can explain the strange disappearance of Schaunard's purse: they look at one another in amazement.*)

STREET URCHINS
Do you think they come from here?

MUSETTA (*to the waiter*)
Give the bill right here to me.

GIRLS, STUDENTS
No! from there!

STREET URCHINS
They are coming from the right!

GIRLS, STUDENTS
No, from left!
(*Several windows on the square are opened. Some mothers with their children lean out of the windows.*)

URCHINS
No, from the right!

MUSETTA
(*to the waiter who hands her the bill*)
Thank you!

VENDORS, TOWNSMEN
Clear the roadway!

SEVERAL BOYS
They're coming near!
Soon they'll be here!

MUSETTA
Take the two bills and add them together!

MOTHERS
Don't go too far away!
I told you not to stay!

RAGAZZI

Mamma, voglio veder!
Papà, voglio sentir!

MUSETTA

Paga il signor che stava qui con me!

RODOLFO, MARCELLO,
SCHAUNARD, COLLINE

Paga il signor.

MAMME

Vuoi tacer, la vuoi finir!

RAGAZZI

Vuò veder la Ritirata!

(*La ritirata si avvicina sempre più dalla sinistra.*)

DONNE, BORGHESI

S'avvicinano di qua!

TUTTI

Sì di qua!

RAGAZZI

Come sarà arrivata
la seguiremo al passo!

(*I bottegai e venditori chiudono le loro botteghe, e vengono in strada*)

COLLINE

Paga il signor!

SCHAUNARD

Paga il signor!

MARCELLO

Il signor!

(*Il cameriere presenta i due conti uniti a Musetta*)

MUSETTA

(*ponendo i due conti riuniti sul tavolo al posto d'Alcindoro*)

È dove s'è seduto
ritrovi il mio saluto!

VENDITORI

In quel rullio tu senti la patria maestà!

RODOLFO, MARCELLO,
SCHAUNARD, COLLINE

E dove s'è seduto
ritrovi il suo saluto!

LA FOLLA

Largo, largo, eccoli qua!
In fila!

MARCELLO

Giunge la ritirata!

MARCELLO, COLLINE

Che il vecchio non ci veda
fuggir colla sua preda!

MARCELLO, SCHAUNARD, COLLINE

Quella folla serrata
il nascondiglio appresti!

RODOLFO

Giunge la ritirata!

(*La ritirata militare attraverso la scena.*)

LA FOLLA

Ecco il tambur maggiore!
Più fier d'un antico guerrier!
Il tambur maggior!
Il tambur maggior!

MIMÌ, MUSETTA, RODOLFO,
MARCELLO, SCHAUNARD, COLLINE

Lesti, lesti, lesti!

LA FOLLA

I Zappator, I Zappatori olà!
Ecco il tambur maggior!
La ritiratata è qua!

(*Musetta non potendo camminare perchè ha un solo piede calzato, è alzata a braccia da Marcello e Colline; a folla vedendo Musetta portata trionfalmente, ne prende pretesto per farle clamorose ovazioni: Marcello e Colline con Musetta si mettono in coda alla ritirata: li seguono Rodolfo e Mimì a braccetto e Schaunard col suo corno imboccato; poi studenti e sartine saltellando allegramente, poi ragazzi, borghesi, donne che prendono il passo di marcia: tutta questa folla si allontana dal fondo seguendo a cantando la ritirata militare.*)

LA FOLLA

Eccolo là!
Il bel tambur maggior!
La canna d'or,
tutto splendor!

BOYS
Mommy, please let me stay!
Papa, I want to play!

MUSETTA
And the man who came with me will
pay!

RODOLFO, MARCELLO,
SCHAUNARD, COLLINE
Yes, he will pay!
(*with comic emphasis*)

MOTHERS
Why can't you for once obey!

BOYS
Let us see the men parading!
(*The soldiers are heard approaching
from the left.*)

GIRLS, TOWNSPEOPLE
They are coming up the street!

ALL
Here they come!

STREET URCHINS
When the parade comes past us
Let's fall in step behind it!
(*The shopkeepers and vendors close
their shops, and move into the
streets.*)

COLLINE
(*aside, with comic emphasis*)
Yes, he will pay!

SCHAUNARD
Yes, he will pay!

MARCELLO
He will pay!
(*The waiter presents the two bills, now
added together, to Musetta.*)

MUSETTA
(*takes the two bills together and puts
them at Alcindoro's place at the table*)
And all my pains and trouble
Will cost him more than double!

VENDORS
In this majestic music our country's
glory shines!

RODOLFO, MARCELLO,
SCHAUNARD, COLLINE
And all her pains and trouble
Will cost him more than double!

ALL THE CROWD
Here they come right up the street!
Let's follow!

MARCELLO
Here comes the whole procession.

MARCELLO AND COLLINE
Be sure our benefactor can't see us steal
his angel!

MARCELLO, SCHAUNARD, COLLINE
Such a crowd is ideal,
It won't be hard to dodge him!

RODOLFO
Here comes the whole procession!
(*The soldiers' procession enters from
the left.*)

ALL THE CROWD
The flags are gaily flying!
May ever so proudly they wave!
Hear the fife and drum!
Hear the fife and drum!

MIMI, MUSETTA, RODOLFO, SCHAUNARD,
COLLINE, MARCELLO
Hurry, hurry, hurry!

CROWD
There they are now!
See how they march along!
See how they march along!
The guards are marching by!
(*Musetta, not able to walk, because she
has only one shoe on, is lifted onto
the shoulders of Marcello and Colline, who get ready to join the procession following the soldiers. The
crowd, seeing Musetta carried off triumphantly, bursts into noisy ovations.
Marcello and Colline, with Musetta,
join the line at the end of the procession, while Rodolfo and Mimi,
their arms linked with Schaunard
blowing his horn, follow. Then come
the students and working girls, skip-
ping about merrily, followed by children, townspeople, and women, all
of them marching in time. All the
crowd goes off-stage, following the
retiring soldier's procession.*)

CROWD
See them parade!
The guards are marching by!
Their heads held high,
The pennants fly!

Che guarda, passa, va!
Tutto splendor!
Di Francia è il più bell'uom!
Il bel tambur maggior!
Eccolo là!
Che guarda, passa, va!

RODOLFO, MARCELLO,
SCHAUNARD, COLLINE

Viva Musetta! Cuor biricchin!

Gloria ed onor!
onor e gloria del quartier latin!

(*Alcindoro con un paio di scarpe bene incartocciate ritorna verso il Caffè Momus, cerca inutilmente Musetta e s' avvicina alla tavola: il cameriere che è li presso, prende i conti lasciati da Musetta e cerimoniosamente li presenta ad Alcindoro, il quale vedendo la somma, cade su di una sedia stupefatto, allibito.*)

QUADRO III

La Barriera D' Enfer

Al di là della barriera il boulevard esterno e, nell' estremo fondo, la strada d'Orleans che si perde lontana fra le alte case e la nebbia del febbraio; al di qua, a sinistra, un Cabaret ed il piccolo largo della barriera, a destra il boulevard d' Enfer; a sinistra quello di St. Jacques. A destra pure la imboccatura della via d' Enfer.

Il cabaret ha per insegna il quadro di Marcello "Il passaggio del Mar Rosso," ma sotto invece, a larghi caratteri, vi è dipinto "Al porto di Marsiglia." Ai lati della porta sono pure dipinti a fresco un turco e uno zuavo con una enorme corona d' alloro intorno al fez. Alla parete del cabaret, che guarda verso la barriera, una finestra a pian terreno donde esce un chiarore rossiccio. E il febbraio; la neve è dappertuto.

All' alzarsi della tela c' è nel cielo e sulle case il biancheggiare incerto della primissima alba. Seduti avanti ad un braciere stanno sonnecchiando i Doganieri. La cancellata della barriera è chiusa.

Dietro la cancellata chiusa, battendo i piedi dal freddo e soffiandosi su le mani intirizzite stanno alcuni spazzini.

SPAZZINI

Ohè, là, le guardie . . . Aprite! . . .
Quelli di Gentilly! . . . Siam gli
 spazzini! . . .

(*I Doganieri rimangono immobili*)

Fiocca la neve! . . . Qui s' agghiaccia!

UN DOGANIERE (*sbadigliando*)

Vengo!

(*Va ad aprire; gli Spazzini entrano e si allontanano per la via d' Enfer. Il Doganiere rinchiude la cancellata.*)

(*Dal Cabaret voci allegre e tintinnii di bicchieri che accompagnano il lieto cantare.*)

VOCI INTERNE

Chi nel ber trovò il piacer,
nel suo bicchier!
d'una bocca nell'ardor,
trovò l'amor, trovò l'amor!

MUSETTA (*nel interno*)

Ah!
Se nel bicchiere sta il piacer
in giovin bocca sta l'amor!

VOCI DAL CABARET

Tralleralè, tralleralè!
Eva e Noè!

VOCI.
(*dal boulevard esterno; dal fondo*)

Hopp-là! Hopp-là!

DOGANIERI

Son già le lattivendole!

(*Dal Corpo di Guardia esce il Sergente dei Doganieri, il quale ordina d' aprire la barriera.*)

CARRETTIERI

Hopp-là!

The sabers gleam and shine!
See them pass by!
They march in perfect line!
While pennants proudly fly!
The sabers shine!
The guards are passing by!

RODOLFO, MARCELLO, SCHAUNARD,
COLLINE

Viva Musetta! Queen of our heart!
Glory and pride,

The joy and glory of the whole Montmartre!

(*Alcindoro, with a new pair of shoes wrapped up in paper, enters and goes toward the Café Momus, looking for Musetta. The waiter, standing by the table, takes the bill left by the friends and presents it ceremoniously to Alcindoro, who seeing the amount, slumps into a chair, stunned and dumbfounded.*)

ACT III

The Barrière d'Enfer

Beyond the toll-gate, the outer boulevard, and in the extreme rear, the Orleans Road, which loses itself in the distance, among old houses, and in the February mist. At the left, there is a tavern and the small yard in front of the toll-gate. At the right, the Boulevard d'Enfer, at the left, the Boulevard St. Jacques.

At the left is the entrance to the Rue d'Enfer. As its sign, the tavern displays Marcello's painting "The Passage of the Red Sea," but beneath is inscribed in large letters "At the Port of Marseilles."

On each side of the entrance is a fresco, one of a Turk, the other of a Zouave. The wall of the tavern which faces the toll-gate has a ground-floor window from which light is shining. It is the end of February. Snow is everywhere.

As the curtain rises, the scene is plunged into the uncertainty of the dawn's first light. Seated in front of a brazier are the customs officers, dozing. The toll-gate barrier is closed.

Behind the closed toll-gate stand the street sweepers, stamping their feet with the cold and blowing into their stiff hands.

STREET-SWEEPERS

Wake up! You keepers! Admit us!
(*The custom officers remain motionless.*)
Hey, there!
We have to go to work!
We are the sweepers!

(*stamping their feet*)
Don't keep us waiting!
Hurry up! We are freezing!
TOLL-GATE OFFICIAL (*rising sleepily*)
Coming!
(*Goes to open the gate. The streetsweepers enter and leave by Rue d'Enfer. The toll-gate official closes the barrier again.*)

WOMEN

(*from the tavern; they accompany their singing by clinking their glasses.*)
All the joys of life combine
In love and wine, in love and wine—
Ah!
Glowing lips and glowing wine
Make life divine, make life divine!

MUSETTA'S VOICE
(*from the tavern*)
Ah!—
In glowing lips and glowing wine
All pleasures in this life combine!

MEN (*from the tavern*)
Tralleralley, tralleraley!
Ever and aye!

MILK SELLERS
(*girls*) (*off-stage*)
Hoopla! Hoopla!

CUSTOMS OFFICER
(*From the guardhouse comes the sergeant of the Customs Office, who gives orders to open the gate.*)
The peasant-girls are coming in!
(*tinkling of cart bells*)

CARTERS
Giddap!

LE LATTIVENDOLE

*(Passano per la barriera a dorso di
asinelli e si allontanano per diverse
strade dicendo ai Doganieri)*

Buon giorno!

CONTADINE

(con ceste a braccio)

Burro e cacio!
Polli ed ova!

(Pagano e i Doganieri le lasciano passare)

Voi da che parte andate?
A San Michele!
Ci troverem più tardi?
A mezzodì;

(Si allontanano per diverse strade)

*(Mimì entra guardando attentamente
intorno cercando di riconoscere i
luoghi, ma giunta al primo platano
la coglie un violento accesso di tosse:
riavutasi e veduto il Sergente, gli
si avvicina.)*

MIMÌ

(al Sergente)

Sa dirmi, scusi, qual è l' osteria . . .

(non ricordandone il nome)

Dove un pittor lavora?

SERGENTE

(indicando il Cabaret)

Eccola.

MIMÌ

Grazie.

(esce una fantesca dal Cabaret)

O buona donna, mi fate il favore
di cercarmi il pittore Marcello?
Ho da parlargli. Ho tanta fretta.
Ditegli, piano, che Mimì l'aspetta.

(la fantesca rientra nel Cabaret)

SERGENTE

(ad uno che passa)

Ehi, quel panier!

DOGANIERI

Vuoto!

SERGENTE

Passi.

*(Le campane dell' ospizio Maria Teresa suonano mattutino. È giorno
fatto, giorno d' inverno triste e caliginoso.)*

MARCELLO

*(esce dal Cabaret e con sorpresa vede
Mimì)*

Mimì?!

MIMÌ

Speravo di trovarvi qui.

MARCELLO

È ver, siam qui da un mese
di quell' oste alle spese.
Musetta insegna il canto ai passeggieri,
io pingo quei guerrieri
sulla facciata.
È freddo. Entrate.

MIMÌ

C' è Rodolfo?

MARCELLO

Sì.

MIMÌ

Non posso entrar, no, no!

MARCELLO

Perchè?

MIMÌ

(scoppia im pianto)

O buon Marcello, aiuto!

MARCELLO

Cos' è avvenuto?

MIMÌ

Rodolfo m'ama,
Rodolfo m'ama e mi fugge,
il mio Rodolfo si strugge
per gelosia.
Un passo, un detto . . .
un vezzo, un fior . . .
lo mettono in sospetto.
Onde corrucci ed ire.
Talor la notte fingo di dormire
e in me lo sento fiso
spiarmi i sogni in viso.
Mi grida ad ogni istante:
"non fai per me,
ti prendi un altro amante,
non fai per me!"
Ahimè! Ahimè!
In lui parla il rovello, lo so,
ma che rispondergli, Marcello?

MARCELLO

Quando s'è come voi
non si vive in compagnia.

MILK-SELLERS

(*to the customs officers, who examine and let them pass*)
Good morning!

SIX PEASANT-WOMEN

(*entering with boxes on their arms*)
(*It stops snowing.*)
Cheese and butter!
Eggs and chicken!
(*They pay and go on.*)
Where are you people going?
St. Michael's market!
Then will we see you later?
At twelve o'clock!
At twelve o'clock!
(*They disappear in different directions.*)
(*Mimi enters, looking around carefully, trying to recognize the surroundings, but arriving at the first plane-tree, she is stricken by a violent attack of coughing. Then she recovers, and seeing the sergeant, goes up to him.*)

MIMI (*to the sergeant*)

Excuse me, Sir,—which is the tavern . . .
(*not able to remember the name*)
Where an artist is painting.

SERGEANT

There it is. (*pointing to the tavern*)

MIMI

Thank you.
(*A servant maid comes out of the tavern.*)
Please may I ask you to do me a favor.
Could you find me the painter
  Marcello?
I have to see him.
It's very urgent.
Quietly tell him that Mimi is waiting.
(*The woman re-enters the tavern.*)

SERGEANT

(*to someone who is passing by*)
Eh, what's in the basket!

CUSTOMS OFFICER

Empty!

SERGEANT

Pass it.
(*From the Maria Teresa Hospice the matin sounds. It is full daylight; a winter day, sad and dark.*)

MARCELLO

(*comes from the tavern, surprised*)
Mimi!

MIMI

I am so glad I found you here.

MARCELLO

Yes, for a month we're staying
At this inn without paying.
Musetta sings her songs for the patron's
  enjoyment;
And I found employment
Painting these murals.
It's cold here. Come in now.

MIMI

Is Rodolfo there?

MARCELLO

Yes.

MIMI

Then I cannot go in.

MARCELLO

Why not?

MIMI (*bursts into tears*)

O dear Marcello, help me! I beg you!

MARCELLO

Tell me what happened?

MIMI

Rodolfo loves me,
And yet he deeply distrusts me,
He makes me suffer unjustly,
He is so jealous.
A chance admission,
A step, a word,
Awaken his suspicion
And start his fury sweeping,
At night, when I pretend that I am
  sleeping,
I feel that he is scheming
To know what I am dreaming.
So many times he told me:
"Our love is gone,
Go find another lover,
We can't go on!"
It breaks my heart!
He does not really mean it, it's true,
But what on earth am I to do?

MARCELLO

If you're both so unhappy,
Then you should not live together.

MIMÌ

Dite ben, dite bene.
Lasciarci conviene.
Aiutateci,
Aiutateci voi.
Noi s'è provato più volte
ma invano.
Dite ben, dite ben
lasciarci convien!

MARCELLO

Son lieve a Musetta
ell'è lieve a me
perchè ci amiamo in allegria.
Canti e risa, ecco il fior
d'invariabile amor!

MIMÌ

Fate voi per il meglio.

MARCELLO

Sta ben, sta ben!
Ora lo sveglio.

MIMÌ

Dorme?

MARCELLO

È piombato qui un' ora avanti l'alba,
s'assopì sopra una panca.
Guardate . . .
(va presso alla finestra e fa cenno a
Mimì di guardare. Mimì tossisce)
Che tosse!

MIMÌ

Da ieri ho l'ossa rotte.
Fuggì da me stanotte
dicendomi: "È finita."
A giorno sono uscita
e me ne venni a questa volta.
(osservando Rodolfo nell' interno del
Cabaret)

MARCELLO

Si desta . . .
s' alza, mi cerca . . .
viene . . .

MIMÌ

Ch' ei non mi veda!

MARCELLO

Or rincasate,
Mimì . . . per carità!
Non fate scene qua!

(Spinge dolcemente Mimì verso l' angolo del Cabaret di dove però quasi
subito sporge curiosa la testa.)

RODOLFO

(accorrendo verso Marcello)
Marcello. Finalmente!
Qui niun ci sente.
Io voglio separarmi da Mimì.

MARCELLO

Sei volubil così?

RODOLFO

Già un' altra volta credetti morto il
mio cor,
ma di quegli occhi azzurri allo splendor
esso è risorto.
Ora il tedio l' assal . . .

MARCELLO

E gli vuoi rinnovare il funeral?

(Mimì non potendo udire le parole,
riesce a ripararsi dietro a un platano,
avvicinandosi così ai due amici.)

RODOLFO (con dolore)

Per sempre!

MARCELLO

Cambia metro.
Dei pazzi è l' amor tetro
che lacrime distilla.
Se non ride e sfavilla,
l' amore è fiacco e roco.
Tu sei geloso.

RODOLFO

Un poco.

MARCELLO

Collerico, lunatico,
imbevuto di pregiudizi,
noioso, cocciuto!

MIMÌ (fra sè)

Or lo fa incollerir!
Me poveretta!

RODOLFO

Mimì è una civetta
che frascheggia con tutti.
Un moscardino
di Viscontino le fa l'occhi di triglia.
Ella sgonnella e scopre la caviglia
con un far promettente e
lusinghier.

MIMI

You are right, I must leave him,
I have to confess it.
All I ask of you,
Will you help us decide?
Though we have tried it so often,
It is hopeless!
It is hard, sad and hard
For lovers to part.

MARCELLO

Take me and my Musetta,
She's ideal for me,
Because she always takes me lightly.
Song and laughter are keeping
Our love firm and strong!

MIMI

Will you promise to help us?

MARCELLO

All right, all right!
I'll go and wake him.

MIMI

Wake him?

MARCELLO

He came here very early in the morning
And fell asleep exhausted.
I'll show you.
(*Motions Mimi to look through the window into the tavern. Mimi coughs persistently.*)

MARCELLO

You are ill!

MIMI

I'm weary to exhaustion.
Last night, Rodolfo left me,
And said to me: "It's the end."
That's why I need your help now,
You have always been our friend.

MARCELLO

(*watching Rodolfo inside the tavern*)
He's waking, rising, and calls me.
He's coming . . .

MIMI

Don't let him see me!

MARCELLO

Then it is better, Mimi.
If you go home!
I'll speak to him alone.

(*Marcello leads Mimi gently towards the corner of the tavern, where, however, she lingers and eavesdrops with interest.*)

RODOLFO

(*comes out of the tavern and rushes towards Marcello*)
Marcello, I'll confide it,
Why should I hide it,
I cannot go on living with Mimi!

MARCELLO

Then you want to be free?

RODOLFO

Once more I thought
That our love was faded and past,
But now I know, my love for her will last,
Always and always
Oh, it drives me insane!

MARCELLO

And you want to renew it all again?
(*Mimi, who has been unable to hear the words, re-enters, unobserved, and moves behind a plane tree near where the friends are conversing.*)

RODOLFO

Forever!

MARCELLO

Change your tune then.
A love that's drear and mirthless
Is dull indeed and worthless.
Love without happy laughter,
Is always stale and brittle.
I think you're jealous.

RODOLFO

A little.

MARCELLO

Cantankerous, belligerent,
Full of prejudice and suspicion,
Annoying and stubborn!

MIMI (*to herself*)

Now his temper will flare!
He is so pettish!

RODOLFO

Mimi is so coquettish,
So inanely flirtatious.
Some silly high-brow,
Some titled dandy makes his leering advances.
And she responds with inviting hints and glances
In a promising way that's all too clear.

MARCELLO

Lo devo dir?
Non mi sembri sincer.

RODOLFO

Ebbene, no, non lo son.
Invan, invan nascondo
la mia vera tortura.
Amo Mimì sovra ogni cosa al mondo,
io l'amo.
Ma ho paura,
ma ho paura!
Mimì è tanto malata!
Ogni dì più declina.
La povera piccina
è condannata!

MARCELLO (sorpreso)

Mimì

MIMÌ (fra sè)

Che vuol dire?

RODOLFO

Una terribil tosse
l'esil petto le scuote
già le smunte gote
di sangue ha rosse . . .

MARCELLO

Povera Mimì!

MIMÌ (piangendo)

Ahime, morire?!

RODOLFO

La mia stanza è una tana
squallida . . . il fuoco ho spento.
V'entra e l'aggira il vento
di tramontana.
Essa canta e sorride,
e il rimorso m'assale.
Me cagion del fatale
mal che l'uccide!

MARCELLO

(vorrebbe allontanare Rodolfo)

Che far dunque?

MIMÌ (desolata)

O mia vita!

RODOLFO

Mimì di serra è fiore.
Povertà l'ha sfiorita,
per richiamarla in vita
non basta amor, non basta amor.

MIMÌ (angoscita)

Ahimè Ahimè!
È finita!
O mia vita!
È finita!
Ahimè morir, ahimè morir!

MARCELLO

Oh qual pietà!
Poveretta!
Povera Mimì!
Povera Mimì!
(La tosse e i singhiozzi violenti rivelano
la presenza di Mimì.)

RODOLFO

(vedendola e accorrendo a lei)

Chè! Mimì! Tu qui?
M'hai sentito?

MARCELLO

Ella dunque ascoltava?

RODOLFO

Facile alla paura
per nulla io m'arrovello.
Vien là nel tepor.
(vuol farla entrare nel Cabaret)

MIMÌ

No, quel tanfo mi soffoca.

RODOLFO

Ah, Mimì!
(Rodolfo stringe amorosamente fra le
sue braccia Mimì)
(Dal Cabaret si ode ridere sfacciata-
mente Musetta.)

MARCELLO

È Musetta che ride.
Con chi ride? Ah la civetta!
Imparerai.
(entra furiosamente nel Cabaret.)

MIMÌ

Addio.

RODOLFO (sorpreso)

Che! Vai?

MIMÌ

Donde lieta uscì
al tuo grido d'amore,
torna sola Mimì
al solitario nido.
Ritorna un' altra volta
a intesser finti fior.
Addio, senza rancor.

MARCELLO

Shall I speak out?
You are not quite sincere.

RODOLFO

All right then, no, I am not!
In vain I have been lying,
I unjustly accuse her!
I love Mimi, my love for her is stronger
Than ever!
But I will lose her,
But I will lose her,
Mimi is dreadfully ailing.
Day by day she is failing.
I fear the spark of life has lost its
power!

MARCELLO (surprised)

Mimi?

MIMI (to herself)

Can he mean it?

RODOLFO

Terrible fits of coughing
Shake her fragile existence,
And her brave resistance
Can't last much longer!

MARCELLO

And I never knew!

MIMI (weeping)

Must I die so soon then?

RODOLFO

And my room is a den of poverty,
No fire is going,
Fiercely the wind is blowing,
Ice-cold, relentless!
She is always so cheerful,
But remorse overcomes me.
I have aided the fearful ill
Which destroys her!

MARCELLO

(tries to lead Rodolfo away)

What to do now?

MIMI (in desolation)

It is true then?

RODOLFO

Mimi is like a flower,
Lacking water and sunshine,
But you can't revive a blossom
By love alone, by love alone.

MIMI (anguished)

All is ended!
All is ended!
All I lived for!
All is ended!
I must say good-bye to all I love.

MARCELLO

O wretched fate!
What a pity!
Must she really die?
Must she really die?
(Her cough and violent sobs reveal the
presence of Mimi.)

RODOLFO (rushing to Mimi)

You, Mimi! You here?
You overheard me?

MARCELLO

Then she has overheard you!

RODOLFO

Darling, you must not mind me,
There is no need to worry.
Here come and get warm!
(tries to lead her into the tavern)

MIMI

No, the heat there would smother me!

RODOLFO

Ah, Mimi!
(presses Mimi lovingly into his arms
and caresses her)
(From the tavern Musetta's brazen
laugh is heard.)

MARCELLO

I can tell it's Musetta.
Who is with her?
Wait till I catch you!
This time I'll show you!
(stormily enters the tavern)

MIMI

Good-bye then!

RODOLFO (astonished)

Mimi! You're leaving!

MIMI

Once again I'll return
To my own scentless flowers,
Lonely as once before
To live with all my mem'ries
Through solitary hours
Where longing never ends!
Good-bye then, we part as friends.

Ascolta, ascolta.
Le poche robe aduna che lasciai sparse.
Nel mio cassetto stan chiusi
quel cerchietto d'or,
e il libro di preghiere.
Involgi tutto quanto
in un grembiale e manderò il
    portiere . . .
Bada . . . sotto il guanciale
c'è la cuffietta rosa.
Se vuoi, se vuoi,
se vuoi serbarla a ricordo d'amor!
Addio,
addio senza rancor.

RODOLFO

Dunque è proprio finita!
Te ne vai, te ne vai,
la mia piccina.
Addio sogni d'amor!

MIMÌ

Addio dolce svegliare
alla mattina!

RODOLFO

Addio sognante vita
che un tuo sorriso acqueta!

MIMÌ (sorridendo)

Addio rabbuffi e gelosie.
Addio sospetti . . .

RODOLFO

Baci!

MIMÌ

Pungenti amarezze.

RODOLFO

Ch' io da vero poeta
Rimavo con: carezze!

MIMÌ

Soli l'inverno . . .

MIMÌ, RODOLFO

è cosa da morire!

MIMÌ

Soli!

MIMÌ, RODOLFO

Mentre a primavera
c'è compagno il sol.

MIMÌ

C'è compagno il sol!
(Dal Cabaret fracasso di piatti e bic-
    chieri rotti)

MARCELLO (di dentro)

Che facevi? Che dicevi?

MUSETTA (di dentro)

Che vuoi dir?

MARCELLO

Presso al fuoco a quel signore?

MUSETTA

Che vuoi dir?
    (Musetta esce stizzita)

MIMÌ

Niuno è solo l'april.

MARCELLO

(fermandosi sulla porta del Cabaret
    rivolto a Musetta)
Al mio venire hai mutato di colore.

MUSETTA

(con attitudine di provocazione)
Quel signore mi diceva:
ama il ballo, signorina?

RODOLFO

Si parla coi gigli e le rose.

MIMÌ

Esce dai nidi un cinguettio gentile.

RODOLFO

Al fiorir di primavera.

MIMÌ

Al fiorir di primavera.

RODOLFO

C'è compagno il sol!

MIMÌ

C'è compagno il sol!

RODOLFO

Chiacchieran le fontane.

MIMÌ

Chiacchieran le fontane.

MIMÌ, RODOLFO

La brezza della sera
balsami stende
sulle doglie umane.
Vuoi che aspettiam
la primavera ancor?

One thing I ask you!
Gather together the few keepsakes I
    treasure.
There in a box is my locket
And the little cross,
Together with my prayerbook.
Collect the other things I own
And I'll send someone to get them
    tomorrow . . .
Listen—under the pillow
I left my little bonnet.
It's yours, it's yours,
A souvenir of love you'll always recall!
Good-bye then
Good-bye for good and all!

RODOLFO

Then you really will leave me,
Dear Mimi, sweet Mimi,
My own beloved,
Farewell to my dream of love.

MIMI

Farewell awaking together
When dawn is ascending!

RODOLFO

Farewell to romantic dreaming
Which had a happy ending!

MIMI (*smiling*)

Farewell distrust and jealous quarrels!
Farewell suspicions,

RODOLFO

Kisses . . .

MIMI

The sharp sting of sadness,

RODOLFO

Which, like ev'ry true poet
I rhymed with "love" and "gladness"!

MIMI

How sad and hopeless

BOTH

To be alone in winter!

MIMI

Lonely!

BOTH

But when spring returns,
The sun will be our friend.

MIMI

Our consoling friend!
(*Inside the tavern the clatter of broken
    plates and glasses is heard.*)

MARCELLO (*from within*)

What the devil is the meaning—

MUSETTA (*from within*)

That's enough!

MARCELLO

Of your giggling and your gushing?

MUSETTA

That's enough!
(*comes out running*)

MIMI

No-one's lonely in spring.

MARCELLO

(*stopping in the door-way of the tavern, turning to Musetta*)

When I came in I saw how deeply you
    were blushing.

MUSETTA

(*with a provocative attitude*)

That nice gentleman was saying:
"Shall we dance now, Miss Musetta?"

RODOLFO

The roses and lilies are blooming!

MIMI

In ev'ry tree the birds are gaily singing.

RODOLFO

In the glory of the springtime

MIMI

In the glory of the springtime

RODOLFO

No one is alone!

MIMI

No one is alone!

RODOLFO

Brooklets and fountains murmur,

MIMI

Brooklets and fountains murmur,

RODOLFO AND MIMI

The tender evening breezes
Calmly descending
Soothe our grief and sorrow,
We'll part when spring is with us once
    again!!

MUSETTA

Arrossendo rispondeva:
ballerei sera e mattina.

MARCELLO

Quel discorso asconde mire disoneste.

MUSETTA

Voglio piena libertà!

MARCELLO

(*quasi avventandosi contro Musetta*)
Io t'acconcio per le feste!

MUSETTA

Chè mi canti?

MARCELLO

Se ti colgo a incivettire

MUSETTA

Chè mi gridi? Chè mi canti?
All' altar non siamo uniti!

MARCELLO

Bada sotto il mio cappello
non ci stan certi ornamenti.

MUSETTA

Io detesto quegli amanti
Che la fanno da—ah! ah! ah! mariti

MARCELLO

In non faccio da zimbello
ai novizi intraprendenti.

MUSETTA

Fo' all'amor con chi mi piace!
non ti garba?
fo' all'amor con chi mi piace!

MARCELLO

Ve n'andate? Vi ringrazio:
or son ricco divenuto.
Vana frivola civetta!

MUSETTA

Musetta se ne va, si, se ne va!

MUSETTA, MARCELLO

Vi saluto.

MUSETTA

Signor, addio.
Vi dico con piacer!

MARCELLO

Son servo e me ne vò!

MUSETTA

Pittore da bottega!

MARCELLO

Vipera!

MUSETTA

Rospo! (*parte*)

MARCELLO

Strega! (*rientra nel Cabaret*)

MIMÌ

Sempre tua per la vita.

RODOLFO

Ci lascieremo . . .

MIMÌ

Ci lascieremo
alla stagion dei fior . . .

RODOLFO

Alla stagion dei fior.

MIMÌ

Vorrei che eterno durasse il verno!

MIMÌ, RODOLFO

Ci lascierem alla stagion dei fior!

QUADRO IV
IN SOFFITTA

*Marcello sta ancora dinanzi al suo cav-
alletto, come Rodolfo sta seduto al
suo tavolo: vorrebbero persuadersi l'
un l' altro che lavorano indefessa-
mente, mentre invece non fanno che
chiacchierare.*

MARCELLO

(*continuando il discorso*)
In un coupè?

RODOLFO

Con pariglia e livree.
Mi salutò ridendo. Tò, Musetta!
Le dissi:—e il cuor?—"Non batte o
non lo sento grazie al velluto che il
copre."

MARCELLO

(*sforzandosi di ridere*)
Ci ho gusto davver.

MUSETTA

And I was blushing when I answered
"There is nothing I'd like better!"

MARCELLO

Sure as fate I know you're up to something shady!

MUSETTA

Liberty is what I want!

MARCELLO

(*almost hurling himself upon Musetta*)
You'll be sorry, my dear lady,

MUSETTA

Why this shouting?

MARCELLO

If I catch you gallivanting!

MUSETTA

Stop your raving! Stop your ranting!
We are not yet married people!

MARCELLO

Do you think you can deceive me
With that feeble-minded fellow.

MUSETTA

I detest that sort of lover
Who behaves just like, hahaha, a
husband!

MARCELLO

I am on to you, believe me,
You don't know your friend Marcello.
Shameless superficial hussy!

MUSETTA

I behave the way I want to!
Don't you like it?
I'll behave the way I want to!

MARCELLO

Are you leaving? I am grateful!
What a lucky stroke of fortune!

MUSETTA

Musetta says good-day, and goes away!

MUSETTA AND MARCELLO

I'm delighted. (*ironically*)

MUSETTA

Good-bye, sir,

MUSETTA AND MARCELLO

The pleasure's mine, good-bye!

MUSETTA

You vulgar shanty painter,

MARCELLO

Jezebel!

MUSETTA

Bull-frog! (*exits*)

MARCELLO

Hell-cat! (*enters the tavern.*)

MIMI

I am yours forever!

RODOLFO

We'll wait till springtime.

MIMI

We'll wait till spring
Before we say good-bye . . .

RODOLFO

Before we say good-bye . . .

MIMI

If only winter would last forever.

BOTH

We'll part when spring is here again!

ACT IV
In the Garret

*Marcello again is standing before his
easel, and Rodolfo is seated at his
table. One tries to convince the other
that he is working hard, while they
actually do nothing but chat.*

MARCELLO

(*continuing the conversation*)

Was that to-day?

RODOLFO

In a handsome coupé.
Smiling, she waved a greeting.
"Well! Musetta," I asked her,
"How's your heart?"
"It's not beating, or I can't feel it,
Buried so deeply in velvet."

MARCELLO (*forcing a laugh*)

I'm happy to hear that,
I'm happy indeed!

RODOLFO (*fra sè*)
(Loiola va. Ti rodi e ridi.)
(*ripiglia il lavoro*)

MARCELLO

Non batte? Bene!—Io pur vidi . . .
(*dipinge a gran colpi di pennello*)

RODOLFO

Musetta?

MARCELLO

Mimì.

RODOLFO (*trasalisce*)
L' hai vista? Oh guarda!

MARCELLO

Era in carrozza
vestita come una regina.

RODOLFO

Evviva. Ne son contento.

MARCELLO (*fra sè*)
(Bugiardo, si strugge d' amor.)

RODOLFO

Lavoriam.

MARCELLO

(*Si mettono al lavoro.*)
Lavoriam.

RODOLFO

(*getta la penna*)
Che penna infame!
(*estrae dalla tasca un nastro di seta e
lo bacia*)

MARCELLO

(*getta il pennello*)
Che infame pennello!

RODOLFO

O Mimì tu più non torni.
O giorni belli,
piccole mani, odorosi capelli . . .

MARCELLO

Io non so come sia che
il mio pennello lavori
e impasti colori
contro voglia mia.

RODOLFO

Collo di neve! Ah! Mimì!
Mia breve gioventù!

MARCELLO

Se pingere mi piace o cieli, o terre,
o inverni, o primavere,
egli mi traccia
due pupille nere,
e una bocca procace.
E n'esce di Musetta il viso ancor . . .

RODOLFO

(*dal cassetto del tavolo leva la cuffietta
di Mimì*)
E tu, cuffietta lieve,
che sotto il guancial
partendo ascose,
tutta sai la nostra felicità.
Vien sul mio cuor, sul mio cuor morto,
ah vien, ah vien sul mio cuor;
poichè è morto amor.

MARCELLO

E n' esce di Musetta
il viso tutto vezzi
e tutto frode.
Musetta intanto gode
e il mio cuor vile la chiama,
  la chiama,
e aspetta il vil mio cuor.

RODOLFO

(*pone sul cuore la cuffietta*)
Che ora sia?

MARCELLO

L' ora del pranzo di ieri.

RODOLFO

E Schaunard non torna?
(*Entrano Schaunard e Colline: il primo
porta quattro pagnotte e l'altro un
cartoccio*)

SCHAUNARD

Eccoci.
(*Depone quattro pagnotte sulla tavola.*)

RODOLFO E MARCELLO

Ebben?

MARCELLO (*con sprezzo*)
Del pan?

COLLINE

(*mostrando un' aringa*)
È un piatto degno di Demostene:
un' aringa . . .

RODOLFO (*to himself*)

(A brazen lie! He's trying to fool me!)
(*resumes his work*)

MARCELLO

Not beating? Splendid!
Guess whom I saw!
(*paints with long strokes of his brush*)

RODOLFO

Musetta?

MARCELLO

Mimi.

RODOLFO

(*startled, stops writing*)

You saw her? Oh, really!

MARCELLO

Dressed like a princess
And riding in a smart-looking carriage.

RODOLFO

That's spendid! I'm glad to hear it!

MARCELLO (*to himself*)

(Not one word he's saying is true.)

RODOLFO

Let us work!

MARCELLO

Let us work!
(*Both resume their work.*)

RODOLFO

This pen is dreadful!
(*throws his pen away*)

MARCELLO

Impossible paint-brush!
(*throws the brush away*)
(*Marcello takes a ribbon from his
pocket and kisses it.*)

RODOLFO

Ah, Mimi, I can't forget you,
Oh golden mem'ry, joys shared
together!
Glorious days departed . . .

MARCELLO

Somehow lately my paint-brush
Has become so capricious
And does as it wishes
All against my will.

RODOLFO

Gone forever! Ah, Mimi!
My fleeting dream of love!

MARCELLO

Whenever I begin to paint a sunset,
The sky, or changing season,
I find it tracing
For some unknown reason,
Two dark eyes and two mocking lips,
The likeness of Musetta, time again!

RODOLFO

(*takes Mimi's bonnet from the table
drawer*)

Ah,—dear little bonnet,
She once gave to me,
As parting remembrance,
You know all, our moments of blinding
joy!
Come to my heart, console my sorrow,
Ah, come, console my lonely heart,
Console my lonely heart!

MARCELLO

Ah, vision of Musetta
With all her charming grace,
So lovely and faithless.
While she enjoys her pleasure,
My forsaken heart keeps calling her
name,
My lonely heart,
My sad and lonely heart!

RODOLFO

(*presses the bonnet to his heart*)

What is the time?

MARCELLO

Time for our yesterday's dinner!

RODOLFO

Not a sign of Schaunard?
(*Schaunard and Colline enter. The former carries four rolls, the latter a
paper bag.*)

SCHAUNARD

Here we are.

RODOLFO

What's that?

MARCELLO

Let's see!
(*Schaunard puts the rolls on the table.*)

MARCELLO (*disdainfully*)

Just bread?

COLLINE

(*opens the bag and extracts a herring
from it*)

A platter worthy of Demosthenes!
Have a herring!

SCHAUNARD
. . . salata.

COLLINE
Il pranzo è in tavola.

MARCELLO
(*fingendo d'assistere ad un lauto pranzo*)
Questa è cuccagna da Berlingaccio.

SCHAUNARD
(*pone il cappello di Colline sulla tavola e vi colloca dentro una bottiglia d' acqua*)
Or lo Sciampagna mettiamo in ghiaccio.

RODOLFO
(*a Marcello, offrendogli del pane*)
Scelga, o Barone, trota o salmone?

MARCELLO (*a Schaunard*)
Duca, una lingua di pappagallo?

SCHAUNARD
Grazie, m' impingua,
Stasera ho un ballo.
(*Colline ha mangiato e si alza.*)

RODOLFO (*a Colline*)
Già sazio?

COLLINE (*con importanza*)
Ho fretta.
Il Re m'aspetta.

MARCELLO
C'è qualche trama?

RODOLFO
Qualche mister?

SCHAUNARD
Qualche mister?

MARCELLO
Qualche mister?

COLLINE
Il Re mi chiama
al minister.

SCHAUNARD
Bene!

MARCELLO
Bene!

RODOLFO
Bene!

COLLINE
(*con aria di protezione*)
Però
vedrò, vedrò . . . Guizot!

SCHAUNARD (*a Marcello*)
Porgimi il nappo!

MARCELLO
(*gli dà l'unico bicchiere*)
Sì! Bevi, io pappo!

SCHAUNARD
Mi sia permesso
al nobile consesso . . .

RODOLFO, COLLINE
(*interrompendolo*)
Basta!

COLLINE
Che decotto!

MARCELLO
Fiacco! Leva il tacco.

COLLINE
Dammi il gotto.

SCHAUNARD (*ispirato*)
M'ispira irresistibile
l'estro della romanza . . .

RODOLFO (*urlando*)
No!

MARCELLO
No!

COLLINE
No!

SCHAUNARD (*arrendevole*)
Azione coreografica allora?

RODOLFO, MARCELLO, COLLINE
Sì sì! . . .

SCHAUNARD
La danza con musica vocale!

COLLINE
Si sgombrino le sale!
(*Portano da un lato tavolo e le sedie e si dispongono a ballare.*)
Gavotta.

MARCELLO
Minuetto.

RODOLFO
Pavanella.

SCHAUNARD
Fandango.

SCHAUNARD
It's pickled!

COLLINE
To tempt an epicure.

MARCELLO
(*pretending to have a splendid meal*)
This is a banquet fit for a Caesar.

SCHAUNARD
(*puts Colline's hat on the table and places a bottle of water in it*)
Put the Champagne to cool in the freezer.

RODOLFO
(*to Marcello, offering him bread*)
Choose, worthy lordship, oysters or salmon?

MARCELLO (*to Schaunard*)
Baron, will you sample this breast of parrot?

SCHAUNARD
No, sir, it's fatt'ning.
I'm sorry, I dare not.
(*Colline, who has gulped down his bread, rises.*)

RODOLFO (*to Colline*)
All finished?

COLLINE
(*with importance and dignity*)
I'm rushing. The King expects me!

MARCELLO
The King expects you?

RODOLFO
What do you mean?

SCHAUNARD
What do you mean?

MARCELLO
What do you mean?

COLLINE
The King has named me Lord Premier!

SCHAUNARD
Splendid!

MARCELLO
Splendid!

RODOLFO
Splendid!

COLLINE (*patronizingly*)
This is the start of my career!

SCHAUNARD (*to Marcello*)
Drink to his meeting!

MARCELLO
(*gives him the glass*)
You do it, I'm eating!

SCHAUNARD
Have I permission
To drink to your commission?

RODOLFO AND COLLINE
(*interrupting him*)
Stop it!

COLLINE
Silly asses!

MARCELLO
Idiot? Stop this nonsense!

COLLINE
Pass the glasses!

SCHAUNARD (*inspired*)
I know a thrilling serenade
Which I'm anxious to offer!

RODOLFO (*howling*)
No!

MARCELLO
No!

COLLINE
No!

SCHAUNARD (*yielding*)
Perhaps the classic dance would amuse you?

RODOLFO, MARCELLO, COLLINE
That's it!

SCHAUNARD
Some dances with vocal orchestrations!

COLLINE
But first the preparations!
(*carrying table and chairs out of the way, they get ready to dance*)

COLLINE
Gavotte.

MARCELLO
Minuet.

RODOLFO
Pavanella.

SCHAUNARD
Fandango!

COLLINE
Propongo la quadriglia.

RODOLFO
Mano alle dame.

COLLINE
Io detto.
(*improvvisando, batte il tempo con comica importanza*)

SCHAUNARD
Lal-le-ra, lal-le-ra!
RODOLFO (*galante a Marcello*)
Vezzosa damigella,

MARCELLO
(*con modestia, imitando la voce femminile*)
Rispetti la modestia.
(*con voce naturale*)
La prego.

SCHAUNARD
Lallera, lallera, lallera!
(*Rodolfo e Marcello ballano la quadriglia*)
Lallera, lallera, lallera!

MARCELLO
COLLINE (*dettando le figure*)
Balancez.

SCHAUNARD (*provocante*)
Prima c'è il *Rond*.

COLLINE
No, bestia!!

SCHAUNARD
Che modi da lacchè!

COLLINE (*prende le molle*)
Se non erro lei m' oltraggia.
Snudi il ferro!

SCHAUNARD (*prende la paletta*)
Pronti. Assaggia.
(*mettendosi in posizione per battersi*)
Il tuo sangue io voglio ber!

COLLINE
Un di noi qui si sbudella.

SCHAUNARD
Apprestate una barella.

COLLINE
Apprestate un cimiter.

RODOLFO, MARCELLO
Mentre incalza la tenzone
gira e balza Rigodone.
(*Si spalanca l' uscio ed entra Musetta in grande agitazione.*)

MARCELLO (*colpito*)
Musetta!
(*con viva ansietà attorniano Musetta*)

MUSETTA
C' è Mimì . . . (*ansimante*)
C' è Mimì che mi segue e che sta male.

RODOLFO
Ov' è?

MUSETTA
Nel far le scale
più non si resse.
(*Si vede, per l' uscio aperto. Mimì seduta sul più alto gradino della scala.*)

RODOLFO
Ah!
(*Si precipita verso Mimì. Marcello accorre anche lui.*)

SCHAUNARD (*a Colline*)
Noi
accostiam quel lettuccio.
(*ambedue portano innanzi il letto*)

RODOLFO
(*coll' aiuto di Marcello porta Mimì fino al letto sul quale la mette distesa*)
Là. Da bere.
(*Musetta accorre col bicchiere dell' acqua e ne dà un sorso a Mimì.*)

MIMÌ
Rodolfo!

RODOLFO
Zitta, riposa.

MIMÌ
O mio Rodolfo,
Mi vuoi qui con te?

COLLINE
And now quadrille positions.

RODOLFO
Please choose your ladies.

COLLINE
Get ready.
(*Improving, he beats the time with comical importance.*)

SCHAUNARD
Lal-le-ra, la-le-ra, lal-le-ra, lá,
   lal-le-ra, lal-le-ra, lal-le-ra, lá.

RODOLFO
(*accosting Marcello, he bows very low, offering his arm*)
Permit me, gracious lady.

MARCELLO
(*modestly, imitating a woman's voice*)
Oh, dear, I'm so embarrassed.
(*with his natural voice*)
With pleasure.

SCHAUNARD
Lallera, lallera, lallera, la.
(*Rodolfo and Marcello are dancing the quadrille.*)

MARCELLO
Lallera, lallera, lallera, la.

COLLINE
(*calls the dance figures*)
Balancez!

SCHAUNARD (*protesting*)
First comes the Round.

COLLINE
No! Jackass!
(*Rodolfo and Marcello continue dancing.*)

SCHAUNARD
You dance like a clod!

COLLINE (*offended*)
I believe you slur my honor.
Here's my challenge!
(*runs to the stove and grabs the tongs*)

SCHAUNARD
(*takes the palette from the fire-place*)
Ready! (*spoken*) On guard!
(*going into duelling position*)
I shall tear you limb from limb!

COLLINE
One of us must die this moment!

SCHAUNARD
Get a hearse for my opponent.

COLLINE
Better dig a grave for him.

RODOLFO AND MARCELLO
While the duel is advancing
Let's continue with our dancing.
(*The door opens wide and Musetta enters in a state of great agitation.*)

MARCELLO (*noticing her*)
Musetta!
(*All gather anxiously around Musetta.*)

MUSETTA (*with choked voice*)
It's Mimi.
It's Mimi, she came with me and is ill.

RODOLFO
Mimi?

MUSETTA
The many stairs were too great an effort.
(*Through the open door Mimi is seen sitting on the highest step of the stairs.*)

RODOLFO
Ah!
(*Rushes toward Mimi. Marcello follows him.*)

SCHAUNARD (*to Colline*)
Move the bed a little nearer.
(*Both move the bed forward.*)

RODOLFO
There. Some water.
(*Rodolfo and Marcello support Mimi and lead her to the bed.*)

MIMI
Rodolfo!
(*Musetta hurries to bring a glass of water, and makes Mimi drink a sip.*)

RODOLFO
Careful, that's better.

MIMI
Oh, my Rodolfo!
May I stay here with you?

RODOLFO

Ah! mia Mimì,
Sempre, sempre!

MUSETTA

(a Marcello, Schaunard e Colline,
  piano)
Intesi dire che Mimì fuggita
dal Viscontino, era in fin di vita.
Dove stia? Cerca, cerca . . .
  la veggo passar per via . . .
trascinandosi a stento.
Mi dice: "Più non reggo . . .
Muoio, lo sento . . .
Voglio morir con lui! forse
  m' aspetta . . . "

MARCELLO

(fa cenno di parlar piano)
Sst.

MIMÌ

Mi sento assai meglio . . .
lascia ch' io guardi intorno.

MUSETTA

"M'accompagni, Musetta?" . . .

MIMÌ

(con dolce sorriso)
Ah come si sta bene qui!
(alzandosi un poco e riabbracciando
  Rodolfo)
Si rinasce, si rinasce.
Ancor sento la vita qui.
No, tu non mi lasci più!

RODOLFO

Benedetta bocca
Tu ancor mi parli!

MUSETTA

Che ci avete in casa?

MARCELLO

Nulla!

MUSETTA

Non caffè? Non vino?

MARCELLO

Nulla! Ah! miseria!

SCHAUNARD (a Colline)

Fra mezz' ora è morta!

MIMÌ

Ho tanto freddo!
Se avessi un manicotto!
Queste mie mani riscaldare
non si potranno mai?   (tosse)

RODOLFO

(prende nelle sue le mani di Mimì,
  riscaldandogliele)
Qui, nelle mie! Taci!
Il parlar ti stanca.

MIMÌ

Ho un po' di tosse!
Ci sono avvezza.
(Vedendo gli amici di Rodolfo, li
  chiama per nome: essi accorrono
  premurosi presso Mimì)
Buon giorno Marcello,
Schaunard, Colline . . . buon giorno.

(sorridendo)
Tutti qui, tutti qui
sorridenti a Mimì.

RODOLFO

Non parlar, non parlar.

MIMÌ

Parlo pian, non temere.
(facendo cenno a Marcello di appres-
  sarsi)
Marcello date retta:
è assai buona Musetta.

MARCELLO

Lo so, lo so.

MUSETTA

(si leva gli orecchini e li porge a Marcello)
A te, vendi, riporta
qualche cordial—manda un
  dottore! . . .

RODOLFO

Riposa.

MIMÌ

Tu non mi lasci?

RODOLFO

No. No.
(Mimì poco a poco si assopisce: Rodolfo prende una scranna e siede presso
al letto.)

RODOLFO

Ah, dear Mimi,
Now and always!

MUSETTA

(*pulls the others away, and says softly
to them*)

I heard the rumor
That Mimi deserted her wealthy Count,
And now was nearly dying.
I went out, hoping, searching . . .
I found her at last to-day.
Pale and weak with exhaustion,
She whispered, "I can't bear it . . .
I'm dying! I feel it,
I want to die near him,
He may be waiting . . ."

MARCELLO

(*to Musetta, so she will lower her
voice*)

Hush!

MIMI

I'm feeling much better.
Just let me look around a little.

MUSETTA

Will you take me, Musetta?

MIMI (*with a sweet smile*)

Ah, it is good to be with you!
(*rising a little and embracing Rodolfo
again*)

I am happy, I am happy.
At last I am with you again
Ah, my love stay close to me!

RODOLFO

Just to hear your voice again,
To have you near me!

MUSETTA

Could we give her something?

MARCELLO

Nothing!

MUSETTA

Any wine or coffee?

MARCELLO

Nothing! Only mis'ry!

SCHAUNARD
(*sadly to Colline*)

She won't live an hour.

MIMI

How cold I am!
I wish I had a muff.
When will these ice-cold hands of mine
Ever get warm again? (*Coughs.*)

RODOLFO

(*takes Mimi's hands into his, warming
them for her*)

Come, let me warm them,
Don't try to speak, my darling.

MIMI

You must not worry!
I'm used to coughing.
(*Seeing the friends of Rodolfo, calling
them by name. They rush to her
eagerly.*)

How are you, Marcello,
Schaunard, Colline, how are you?
(*smiling*)

Here you are, all you three
Smiling welcome to me.

RODOLFO

You must rest, do not talk.

MIMI

Only softly, I promise.
(*making a sign to Marcello to come
nearer*)

Marcello, let me tell you:
Your Musetta is good.

MARCELLO

I know, I know.

MUSETTA

(*takes off her earrings and hands them
to Marcello*)

Take these, sell them,
And buy whatever will help.
Go for the doctor!

RODOLFO

Lie quiet.

MIMI

You will not leave me?

RODOLFO

No! No!
(*Mimi gradually becomes drowsy. Rodolfo takes a chair and sits down near
the bed.*)

MUSETTA

Ascolta!
Forse è l' ultima volta
che espresso ha un desiderio,
    poveretta!
Pel manicotto io vo. Con te verrò.

MARCELLO

Sei buona, o mia Musetta.
(*Musetta e Marcello partono frettolosi.*)

COLLINE

(*mentre Musetta e Marcello parlavano
    si è levato il pastrano*)
Vecchia zimarra, senti,
io resto al pian, tu ascendere il sacro
    monte or devi.
Le mie grazie ricevi.
Mai non curvasti il logoro
dorso ai ricchi ed ai potenti.
Passar nelle tue tasche
come in antri tranquilli
filosofi e poeti.
Ora che i giorni lieti
fuggir, ti dico addio
fedele amico mio,
addio, addio.
(*Colline fattone un involto se lo pone
    sotto il braccio, ma vedendo Schau-
    nard, gli dice sottovoce*)
Schaunard, ciascuno per diversa via
mettiamo insieme due atti di pietà;
io . . . questo!
(*gli mostra la zimarra che tiene sotto
    il braccio*)
E tu . . .
lasciali soli là! . . .

SCHAUNARD (*commosso*)

Filosofo, ragioni!
È ver! . . . Vo via!
*Si guarda intorno, e per giustificare
    la sua partenza prende la bottiglia
    dell' acqua e scende dietro Colline
    chiudendo con precauzione l' uscio.*)

MIMÌ

(*apre gli occhi*)
Sono andati? Fingevo di dormire
perchè volli con te sola restare.
Ho tante cose che ti voglio dire
o una sola, ma grande come il
mare,

come il mare profonda ed
    infinita . . .
Sei il mio amor e tutta la mia
    vita.

RODOLFO

Ah! Mimì, mia bella Mimì.

MIMÌ

Son bella ancora?

RODOLFO

Bella come un' aurora.

MIMÌ

Hai sbagliato il raffronto.
Volevi dir: bella come un tramonto.
"Mi chiamano Mimì
(*Come eco*)
mi chiamano Mimì
il perchè non so."

RODOLFO

(*intenerito e carezzevole*)
Tornò al nido la rondine e cinguetta.
(*Si leva di dove l' aveva riposta, in sul
    cuore, la cuffietta di Mimì e gliela
    porge.*)

MIMÌ (*raggiante*)

La mia cuffietta. Ah!
(*Tende a Rodolfo la testa, questi le
    mette la cuffietta.*)
Te lo rammenti quando sono entrata
la prima volta, là?

RODOLFO

Se lo rammento!

MIMÌ

Il lume s'era spento . . .

RODOLFO

Eri tanto turbata!
Poi smarristi la chiave . . .

MIMÌ

E a cercarla
tastoni ti sei messo!

RODOLFO

E cerca, . . . cerca . . .

MUSETTA

Marcello!
This may be the last time
That Mimi ever expresses a desire!
I'll go and buy the muff.
You come with me.

MARCELLO

How good you are, Musetta.
(*Musetta and Marcello leave
hurriedly.*)

COLLINE

(*While Marcello and Musetta are talk-
ing he takes off his overcoat.*)
Faithful companion, listen,
I must remain, you journey to higher,
better regions,
Take my grateful allegiance.
Neither to wealth nor temporal power
Have you ever yielded.
Hidden deep in your pockets,
Cozily there have rested
Philosophers and poets.
Now that our happy days have gone by,
I bid you farewell, (*with emotion*)
Ever faithful old companion.
Farewell, farewell.
(*He rolls up his coat, puts it under his
arm and starts to leave, but seeing
Schaunard, he goes to him, pats his
shoulder and says sadly.*)
Schaunard,
Each of us in a diff'rent way
Can now accomplish a kindness of his
own,
(*pointing to his overcoat*)
I this one. And you . . .
Let them stay here alone.

SCHAUNARD (*moved*)

A logical conclusion!
You're right. I'll go.
(*Schaunard looks around and in order
to justify his leaving, he takes the
water bottle and leaves after Colline,
gently closing the door.*)
(*Mimi opens her eyes, seeing that all
have left, extends her hand toward
Rodolfo, which he kisses lovingly.*)

MIMI

Have they gone now?
I was not really sleeping.
To make them leave us,
I only was pretending.
So many things are in my heart to tell
you,

Or just one, which is true and never-
ending.
As the sky is eternal there above you,
So is my love, and I will always love
you!

RODOLFO

Ah, Mimi, my lovely Mimi!

MIMI

Am I really still lovely?

RODOLFO

Fair as sunshine at dawning!

MIMI

A mistaken defining!
You should have said:
Fair as sunset declining.
"I'm always called Mimi,
(*like an echo*)
I'm always called Mimi,
But I don't know why . . ."

RODOLFO

(*in a tender and caressing tone*)
Home to her nest came the weary little
swallow.
(*He takes the bonnet from where he
had kept it, close to his heart, and
gives it to Mimi.*)

MIMI

(*Cheerfully, turns her head to Rodolfo.
He puts the bonnet on it.*)
My little bonnet, my little bonnet! Ah!
Do you remember how by chance I
came here
The first time that we met?

RODOLFO

Do I remember!

MIMI

The wind blew out the candles . . .

RODOLFO

And you were so embarrassed!
Then your door-key was missing.

MIMI

You tried to find it
In spite of the darkness!

RODOLFO

We looked, and looked . . .

MIMÌ

Mio bel signorino
posso ben dirlo adesso,
lei la trovò assai presto.

RODOLFO

Aiutavo il destino.

MIMÌ

Era buio, e il mio rossor non si
    vedeva . . .
"Che gelida manina . . .
Se la lasci riscaldar! . . ."
Era buio, e la man tu mi
    prendevi . . .

(*Mimì è presa da uno spasimo di soffocazione; lascia ricadere il capo,
sfinita.*)

RODOLFO (*spaventato*)

Oh Dio! Mimì.

(*In questo momento Schaunard ritorna: al grida di Rodolfo accorre presso Mimì.*)

SCHAUNARD

Che avvien?

MIMÌ

(*apre gli occhi e sorride per rassicurare
Rodolfo e Schaunard*)

Nulla . . . Sto bene.

RODOLFO

Zitta per carità.

(*la adagia sul cuscino*)

MIMÌ

Sì, sì perdona.
Or sarò buona.

(*Musetta, Marcello, poi Colline. Musetta porta un manicotto e Marcello
una boccetta.*)

MUSETTA (*a Rodolfo*)

Dorme?

RODOLFO

Riposa.

MARCELLO

Ho veduto il dottore!
Verrà; gli ho fatto fretta.
Ecco il cordiale.

(*Prende una lampada a spirito, la pone
sulla tavola e l' accende.*)

MIMÌ

Chi parla?

MUSETTA

(*si avvicina a Mimì e le porge il manicotto*)

Io, Musetta.

MIMÌ

(*aiutata da Musetta si rizza sul letto,
e con gioia quasi infantile prende
il manicotto*)

Oh come è bello e morbido.
Non più, non più
le mani allividite.
Il tepore l' abbellirà.
Sei tu che me lo doni?

MUSETTA (*pronta*)

Sì.

MIMÌ (*a Rodolfo*)

Tu! Spensierato!
Grazie. Ma costerà. Piangi? Sto
    bene . . .
Pianger così perchè? . . .

(*assopendosi a poco a poco*)

Qui . . . amor . . . sempre con te! . . .
Le mani . . . al caldo . . . e . . .
    dormire.   (*silenzio*)

RODOLFO (*a Marcello*)

Che ha detto il medico?

MARCELLO

Verrà.

MUSETTA

(*fa scaldare la boccetta alla lampada
a spirito, e quasi inconsciamente mormora una preghiera*)

Madonna benedetta,
fate la grazia a questa poveretta
che non debba morire.

(*interrompendosi, a Marcello*)

Qui ci vuole un riparo
perchè la fiamma sventola.

(*Marcello mette un libro ritto sulla
tavola formando paravento alla
lampada.*)

Così.

(*ripiglia la preghiera*)

E che possa guarire.
Madonna santa, io sono
indegna di perdono,
mentre invece Mimì
è un angelo del cielo.

RODOLFO

Io spero ancora.
Vi pare che sia grave?

MUSETTA

Non credo.

MIMI

Now my young Lothario,
You may as well admit it,
You found it soon, but you hid it.

RODOLFO

I improved the scenario.

MIMI

In the dark, you could not see how I
was blushing,
"How cold your little hand is . . .
Let me warm it in my own!"
It was dark, and you took my hand in
yours.
(*Gripped by a spasm of coughing, she
lets her head fall back, exhausted.*)

RODOLFO (*terrified*)

Oh God, Mimi!

SCHAUNARD

(*at this moment returning, runs to
Mimi, at the outcry of Rodolfo*)
What's wrong?

MIMI

(*opens her eyes and smiles, reassuring
Rodolfo and Schaunard*)
Nothing . . . I'm better.

RODOLFO

(*putting her back on the pillow*)
Careful, for Heaven's sake!

MIMI

Yes, yes, forgive me,
I'll be good now . . .
(*Musetta and Marcello enter quickly.
Musetta carries a muff, Marcello a
medicine bottle.*)

MUSETTA (*to Rodolfo*)

How is she?

RODOLFO

She's resting.

MARCELLO

I have called at the doctor's.
He'll come. I made it urgent.
Meanwhile, take this—
(*takes a spirit-lamp, puts it on the table
and lights it*)

MIMI

Who is it?

MUSETTA

(*goes to Mimi, and gives her the muff*)
I, Musetta.

MIMI

(*Helped by Musetta, she sits up in bed,
and with almost child-like joy, takes
the muff.*)
Oh, it's so soft and beautiful!
At last, at last,
My hands will get warm now.
This will keep them . . .
So nice and soft . . .
Did you do this for me?

MUSETTA (*quickly*)

Yes.

MIMI

You! What a spendthrift!
Thank you! It costs a lot!
You're crying? I'm better . . .
Why do you weep like this?
(*with a very weak voice*)
I'm here . . . Always with you! . . .
(*fading away more and more*)
My hands are . . . So warm now . . .
I . . . am tired . . .

RODOLFO (*to Marcello*)

What did the doctor say?

MARCELLO

He'll come.

MUSETTA

(*meanwhile, has warmed up the medi-
cine, and while she is engaged in this
action, murmurs a prayer*)
Oh, gracious Virgin Mary,
Bless her, I beg you,
With your boundless mercy,
So she won't have to die
(*interrupts herself, motions to Marcello,
who comes to her and puts a book up-
right on the table, shading the lamp.*)
We must fasten a shade there,
Because the flame is flickering,—
Like this . . .
(*resuming her prayer*)
Oh, please let her recover;
Mother most holy,
I am unworthy of your pardon,
But Mimi is just like an angel from
Heaven.

RODOLFO

I think she's better.
You do not think it's hopeless?

MUSETTA

Of course not.

SCHAUNARD

Marcello, è spirata.

(Intanto Rodolfo si è avveduto che il sole dalla finestra della soffitta sta per battere sul volto a Mimì e cerca intorno come porvi riparo; Musetta se ne avvede e gli indica la sua mantiglia. Rodolfo la ringrazia con uno sguardo, prende la mantiglia, sale su di una sedia e studia il modo di distenderla sulla finestra.)

(Entra Colline che depone del danaro sulla tavola presso a Musetta.)

COLLINE

Musetta, a voi!
Come va?

RODOLFO

Vedi! . . . È tranquilla.

(Si volge verso Mimì: in quel mentre Musetta gli fa cenno che la medicina è pronta.)

(nell' accorrere presso Musetta si accorge dello strano contegno di Marcello e Schaunard che, pieni di sgomento, lo guardano con profonda pietà)

Che vuol dire

quell' andare e venire . . .
quel guardarmi così . . .

MARCELLO

(non regge più, corre a Rodolfo e abbracciandolo stretto a sè con voce strozzata gli mormora)

Coraggio.

RODOLFO

Mimì! . . .

(si precipita al letto di Mimì, la solleva e scuotendola grida colla massima disperazione)

(si getta sul corpo esanime di Mimì)
Mimì! . . .

(Musetta, spaventata corre al letto, getta un grido angoscioso, buttandosi ginocchioni e piangente ai piedi di Mimì dalla parte opposta di Rodolfo —Schaunard si abbandona accasciato su di una sedia, a sinistra della scena Colline va ai piedi del letto, rimanendo atterrito per la rapidità della catastrofe—Marcello singhiozza, volgendo le spalle al proscenio.)

CALA LENTAMENTE IL SIPARIO

SCHAUNARD

Marcello, she's dead . . .

(*A ray of sunshine falls on Mimi's face through the window. Rodolfo notices it and looks for a way to put up a curtain. Musetta points to her cloak. Rodolfo thanks her with a look, takes the cloak, climbs on a chair and tries to drape it across the window.*)

COLLINE

(*enters discreetly, putting the money on the table, near Musetta*)

Musetta, for you!
How is she?

RODOLFO

(*turning, sees Musetta, who motions to him that the medicine is ready. He descends from the chair, but while approaching Musetta he becomes aware of the strange behavior of Marcello and Schaunard.*)

Look, she is asleep.
What is wrong?

You are acting so strangely.
Why look at me like that?

MARCELLO

(*cannot contain himself any longer, rushes to Rodolfo, and exclaims, embracing him*)

Rodolfo!

RODOLFO

(*rushes to the bed, grasps Mimi and cries out in the utmost despair*)

Mimi!

(*throws himself upon the lifeless body of Mimi*)

Mimi!

(*Musetta, terrified, rushes to the bed, with an anguished outcry. Kneeling in tears at the feet of Mimi opposite Rodolfo, Schaunard sinks into a chair, despondent. Colline stands at the bed, remaining stunned by the suddenness of the tragedy; Marcello, sobbing, stands with his back to the audience.*)

END OF THE OPERA